High Tide and the Heron Dived
A TOTNES CHILDHOOD

The War and After

JANET COGGIN

FOLLY ISLAND PRESS

Also by Janet Coggin

The Leaving

McElhinney

Northside

The Spy's Wife

Translation

Love in the Snow by Alexandros Papadiamantis

First published in Great Britain 2012 by Folly Island Press
ISBN 978-0-9528359-1-2
schiffrin.schiffrin@gmail.com
© 2012 Tom Gerhardt and Ingrid Nowlan Gerhardt

Edited by Maria Elena de La Iglesia
Designed by Sue Snell
Author photograph by Lee Godfrey
Printed by Brightsea Press, Exeter, Devon

To the memory of my father, Maurice Coggin
with gratitude for the freedom and care and love he gave to us.

Also for Ingy, Sam, Andrew and Kirsten,
in the hope it may interest you
and perhaps make you laugh a little

High tide and the heron dived when I took the road
Over the border
And the gates
of the town closed as the town awoke

Dylan Thomas
Poem In October

The Wishing Well

About a mile and a half from our house, up a steep stony lane, there was an old wishing-well, covered in ivy and shaded by high hedges and massive oak trees. There was an atmosphere of mystery and ancient magic around it and I never for a moment doubted its secret powers. Whenever we passed by, which was often because my father was a great man for walks, each person would pick an ivy leaf and throw it into the water, silently making a wish.

When the system was first explained to me I couldn't think what to wish for so I whispered (because I knew you weren't supposed to divulge wishes) to my father, 'What did you wish?'

'What I always wish,' he replied. 'That the war would end.'

So from then on I wished it too – thinking it must be a good thing to wish for, if he thought so – but at the same time without the least idea of what 'the war' was. Nobody had ever told me and strangely, for it seems strange now in a different age when children demand to know everything, I never enquired. Perhaps I didn't fully want to know, instinctively preferring ignorance, or perhaps I felt that if someone wanted to tell you something they would, and if they didn't they wouldn't. Either way, 'the war' seemed generally to be a fact of life: something concerning bombs and Jerries and shortages, and only manifested itself now and then. Like the times when I was out walking with my nanny and loud propeller-driven aeroplanes would appear in the sky, passing low overhead; the way she would start bawling out, 'The Jerries, the Jerries!' and pick me up and hurl me into the nearest ditch (regardless of the sharp stones or brambles or even vicious stinging nettles I might land on) hissing after me, 'Don't move! Or the Jerries will get you!'

I used to lie still, obediently, until the planes were gone and the sky clear and innocent again, and then climb out, rubbing my sores, and start looking for her – usually to be found cowering under a clump of bushes. And we would go on together, enjoying our walk, picking hazel nuts from the hedges, or blackberries, or collecting primroses – or whatever it was we were doing – as if nothing had, or ever would again, disturb our peace.

It seemed that everything important – world shattering to me – happened to our family all at once in 1939, when I was three and a half and my sister six, going on seven. That was when our Danish mother, a sort of misty, half-real, almost imaginary character to me for most of my life, decided to leave home and children for a new life*. Also it was when war with Germany was declared, and the same year that my family – now down to us two children, our father and a nanny – moved from our house in Cambridge and set up home in Totnes, a small agricultural market town on the River Dart in Devonshire.

My father had his own theories of child-rearing. He believed that the more you fussed over a child, the more fractious it would become; the more you pampered it the more stupid it would grow to be; the more you threatened it to make it behave well, the more fearful or rebellious it would be; and the more you lectured or forced your own opinion on it, the less the child would think for itself. On the other hand, the more you left it to simply grow and develop in its own way at its own pace, the better chance it had of becoming a reasonable human being.

His own school education had been of the type that believed in forcibly instilling everything into children – from Greek or Latin verbs, to how to speak and behave and what to think. And the school his parents had selected for him, Winchester College, where beatings, bullying and snobbishness were (at that time) the order of the day, had done nothing for him but enrage his sense of decency and justice. He had such a bad opinion of schools in general that when it came to choosing one for us, he did not look so much for a school that would do his children good, as one that he hoped would do the least harm.

Dartington Hall, the school he settled on for us, was unusual to say the least, especially in those days of strict regimentation and conformity. It was the reason we had come to live in Totnes, for it was only two miles out of the town. Locally it was considered more or less a loony bin, for

*Captain Nora Coggin spent most of the war years in Cairo, officially in the First Aid Nursing Yeomanry but possibly in secret work.

the children called the teachers by their Christian names and didn't have to attend classes if they didn't want to. The idea being that they would eventually tire of having nothing to do and find they did actually want to learn things. I suppose it worked quite well in most cases – although I have to admit to being one of the last to voluntarily go into harness. However, this was never considered a problem; learning was hardly top priority in the minds of parents at that time, who were constantly aware, not only of the random bombing raids, but of the ever-present threat of the whole country being invaded and overrun by a cruel and fascist regime. All they wanted was for their children to be happy and free for as long as it might last.

Everyone can remember their first day of school, when they were taken by an apprehensive parent and left in the care of strangers. My recollection though, is of almost immediately, while still outside in the garden, having my attention captured by a gang of ducks, dashing around under everyone's feet. I was shown how to mix cornmeal with water in a big flat bowl and then to scatter it on the grass and watch it being noisily devoured. Then I and some other children were given glass baby-feeding bottles with warm milk to feed some young orphan lambs from the school farm. Seeing for the first time baby lambs at such close range, being able to touch them, feeling them pulling and sucking at the bottles, all the children were enthralled and lost their sense of being in unknown territory. But then I saw our familiar black car driving off along the road, past the school, into the distance and finally disappearing. It was my first experience of panic; suddenly it was the end of the world, I was all alone, deserted.

By the time my anxious father returned, having been summoned on the phone by a teacher, I was happily re-engrossed again, and indignant. 'Why have you come back? I don't want to go home.'

It seems there was a conspiracy among adults to withhold all information concerning the warring world outside. So it was not surprising that none of us had the slightest idea of what was going on. There was a children's street song at the time, which we used to sing:

> *Underneath the spreading chestnut tree,*
> *I saw Hitler and he saw me.*
> *All the little birdies tickled his feet,*
> *In the trenches six foot deep.*

Other versions were ruder, of course. But what did they mean? Who was this Hitler, and what on earth was he doing in trenches six foot deep? And of all things, with birds tickling his feet? It was incomprehensible nonsense, but it didn't bother us much. We just sang it because we knew it.

For us, the books that were read to us at school during the lunch rest breaks, were much more exciting than the present wartime reality. Mostly they were rousing stories of the lives and deeds of great men, kings and heroes. One by one we went through *King Arthur, Alexander the Great, Olaf the Viking King, Julius Caesar, Robin Hood, Ivanhoe,* not to mention a whole bevy of Norse and Homeric heroes of ancient myth and legend, interspersed with *The Hobbit, Robinson Crusoe, Treasure Island* and various adventures of the *Swallows and Amazons.* Of course we were all fired with enthusiasm for these brave and often god-like characters, and we would act out their stories and adventures, inventing our own variations, different each time, for weeks afterwards; dressing up in old curtains and towels and anything we could find, dancing and fighting and pretending to be Rowena, Rebecca and Ivanhoe – or whoever were the current favourites.

Sometimes, quite unaccountably, we played games like 'French and English' where the two sides were enemies. Where the idea came from I don't know, I can only imagine it was a throw down from the times of the Napoleonic Wars. So far, the only fact of the present war that we knew was that the Germans (whoever they were) were the enemy. Now here was this confusing matter about the French (whoever they were) being enemies too; It was too much for any of us to understand, so we just got on with our games and left the grown-ups to sort their own problems out.

Whenever the air raid siren blasted through the air from the town, two miles away, we would come running in from the garden, dive under our desks and sit waiting for the All Clear to sound. Sometimes we could hear aeroplanes going overhead and we would half-dread and half-hope for the sound of an explosion – some kind of exciting action. It seemed as normal a part of school as anything else.

By now private cars were banned on the roads, because all the petrol was needed for the war. For those of us that lived in Totnes, there was a local bus to Dartington three times a day. My father would always be waiting on the Plains (the town square) to walk home with me, over the big stone bridge and up the long, steep hill to where we lived. From the centre of the bridge there was a sort of ramp going down onto an island in the middle of the River Dart. Sometimes, before going home, we would go down on to the island to watch huge barges being built in the narrow strip of water between the sawmills on the quay and the island. Hidden by tall spreading trees, landing barges were being produced as fast as humanly possible, to replace the heavy naval losses at sea. On completion these would be taken down the river by night to Dartmouth and then round to Plymouth, where they would later be used in the D-Day landings on the French coast.

All the local people knew that if the secret got out and became known to the Germans, the town would be bombed flat; but they were proud that Totnes was 'doing its bit' and there was nearly always an admiring audience of adults and children standing around under the trees.

My sister, Ingrid, would come back from school later than I. Maybe she knew a little more of what was going on, what the war meant, because she didn't seem to like air raids and used to feel sick when at night we would go downstairs to the room we called the 'shelter'. We called it this because my father had blacked the windows with sandbags, so that glass wouldn't fly about when the house shook and rattled. He drew the line at using the communal town shelter because he felt sure people would either be having hysterics, or at least coughing and sneezing and spreading germs. Or, horror of horrors, singing to keep cheerful: none of which was his style of dealing with the situation. He had also decided against building a shelter in the garden – those government shelters that came in ready-to assemble corrugated iron kits – because he thought they would be damp and depressing.

I used to enjoy going down to our 'shelter', especially as we were given barley sugar sticks (obtained from the chemist for medicinal purposes and the nearest thing to sweets in those days). And my father would read to us until the All Clear siren sounded – so it all seemed pretty OK to me. Occasionally bombs fell in the distance, out in the fields. Mostly these were dropped by planes that were chasing or being chased and needed to lighten their load in order to fly faster. Once a bomb exploded so loudly and the house shook so violently that I was convinced it had landed right in our garden. No one would believe me and I was very frustrated because they wouldn't let me go out to look – I wanted to see and prove to myself, and everyone else, that I was right. But the next day, I was surprised and disappointed to discover the bomb crater was at least a mile away in a field of cows. It was good to know that no cow had been hit, and even funny to imagine how surprised they must have been. Later, after a few months had passed and the crater filled up with rainwater, there was a pond in the field from which the animals could drink. At which my nanny pointed out triumphantly – for she liked her favourite maxims to be proved correct – that 'it was an ill wind that blew nobody good'.

Nanny Brockbank was her name, and she was my nanny. My sister had had a different nanny when we were in Cambridge but she had not come down to Devon with us; she had joined the Women's Army.

Nanny Brockbank only panicked once in front of my father. That was when a particularly savage-sounding bomb fell not far away and rocked the whole house. He had given her a friendly but firm look and said, 'None of that, please.' And after that she never seemed to feel the need to do it again – in the house anyway. She still continued to yell and throw me into ditches when we were out alone together and planes came overhead (it had become a routine) but when he was around she didn't like to be caught on the wrong footing, for she was properly conscious that she was a 'Norland Nanny'. That is to say, she was trained at the most prestigious establishment for nannies in England and was very proud of it. She even wore a special uniform so there could be no mistaking her status, and was quite sure that her ways were the right ways concerning all children, and that my father had no business to be having his own views on childrearing.

So he was, I think, not exactly cast down when her call-up papers arrived in the post. She had spurned the Land Army and so was requested to report to a munitions factory in the north of England.

I don't remember if I missed her when she left, just as I don't remember if I missed my mother. A neighbour told me years later, when I was older, that she used to hear me crying a lot in the garden at that time, and then after some weeks I had stopped and was a happy child again. I always remembered what nanny Brockbank looked like – short, dark, straightish hair with a fringe. And a nice smile.

And I remembered her sayings:

> *There's none so blind as those who will not see!*
> *Waste not want not!*
> *More haste, less speed!*

There's no such word as can't!
If you don't at first succeed try, try again!

And countless others. She had a store of them and was never at a loss to produce the appropriate one. My father once told me, rather sadly, how very much she had loved me – and I think I must have loved her too, for I always got a good feeling when I looked at a photograph of her. Suddenly she had gone, and life went on.

Father and Two Small Girls

My father was too old to be called for this war against Hitler and fascism. For refusing to take part, he had spent the 1914-18 war in Princeton prison on Dartmoor as a conscientious objector . A young man of twenty or so, just down from St John's College, Cambridge, he had told the judge at his trial, 'I'm not going to kill unless I see a just reason for it. To me, there is nothing that justifies this war; it's about money and political power.' He wrote to the Home Secretary, 'You should make up your mind whether you imprison people for murdering – or for refusing to murder.' In fact there were so many of his Cambridge contemporaries in the same prison that it was called The Settlement, and he often said it was the best time of his life. They produced plays, gave each other lectures and even had a newspaper. But after the war, in which so many young men had died, he found he was very unpopular.

After the war he succumbed to the virulent pneumonia that killed so many people after the war. His father was notified that his life was in danger, but the return telegram stated "Have no son of that name." His mother had died when he was fourteen; now his father disowned him. He hadn't had much family life anyway, having been sent to a Spartan preparatory boarding school at the age of eight; and then on to Winchester College where, in those days, boys were beaten by older boys and by housemasters. And even when he had been at home, in the holidays, he and the other children (one brother and two sisters, all younger) had been kept in a separate part of the house with nannies and governesses, and only brought to see their parents once a day, washed and brushed, to be inspected – or that was how it seemed to him.

And now, with practically no experience at all to guide him, he had found himself responsible for two small girls, at a time when all able, employable women were being called up for war work. So he was left, whether he liked it or not, to his own devices; to cook and wipe bottoms and dry tears and run a home. I imagine it must have been quite a daunting prospect at that period when men weren't expected to know about such things.

Black material was found for all the windows, cut to size, folded and kept on the window sills. Each evening at the appropriate hour given out on the wireless, we would go round the house; my father putting up the 'black out'; we, handing up drawing pins and stretching out the pieces of cloth to make it easier for him. Then we would pull the curtains across the front of it, to hide the ugliness and forget it was there. But if it was not done properly, if so much as a chink of light leaked through, there would be a knock at the door and the voice of the man whose duty it was to check: 'Sorry, but there's light showing through.'

The biggest chore was the garden. The public was urged, 'Dig up your lawns! Dig up your flower beds too! Grow vegetables.' With only a garden fork and spade (none of your modern mechanical gardening aids) it must have been a marathon effort. We became accustomed to seeing our father's tall figure struggling and straining in the garden. Typical children though, we assumed he did it because that's what he like doing. We didn't approve – the lawn was disappearing. Where would we play ?

'In the wilderness, of course,' he said. The wilderness was his name for the overgrown orchard at the end of the garden, because it had been left for decades to grow wild. The grass was waist high (for children) and tangled up with old roots, fallen branches, chamomile and nettles. It was exciting wriggling through, trying to avoid the nettles; leaving a network of tunnels, and then climbing up the rickety old fruit trees and eating the damsons, apples and pears. There were nut trees too, cob nuts, and the two largest pines I have ever seen.

We discovered the remains of an old chicken shed and rushed to my father – 'Why don't we keep hens? We could collect the eggs every day.' But he wouldn't agree. He didn't like hens. More than that, he positively disliked them. He had tried keeping chicken when we had lived in Cambridge, he told us, but had been disgusted by them, When one got sick, all the others pecked it to death. He would never keep hens again. So that was that. Disappointed, we turned our minds to other possibilities. 'What about a kitten?'

He rolled his eyes heavenwards and muttered something like: 'I suppose there'll be no end to this sort of thing,' as if having a presentiment of what years of rearing children might bring. He probably visualised the whole garden being turned into a menagerie.

Determined to start as he meant to go on, he brooked no nonsense. He got to know the pattern of things; regular occurrences. Like when it rained and we stayed in all day, how inevitably we would start quarrelling and whingeing. 'Right,' he would say, 'get your macs and boots on.' His remedy for everything was a walk, regardless of whether it was lashing rain or sleet or worse. And despite our protests we would find ourselves running along behind his long strides. And soon, sure enough we would cease to notice the weather and begin to enjoy the day. As he said, if we all returned soaked through, what did it matter? We could change our clothes, couldn't we? At least he could bear to look at us now that we were cheerful again.

Although I preferred being at home, school was good fun too and I liked to keep a sort of harmonious thread running between the two, so that I went back and forth from one enjoyable situation to another. One time, after I had been kept at home for a week with flu, I had a nasty experience when I returned to school, which quite shook me at the time. It was like when Peter Pan flies back to his home and finds his parents have put bars over his bedroom window and a new baby is in his bed. My incident was nowhere near as bad as that, but nevertheless it came as a shock. What happened was, while I was away a new girl had come to join the class. I didn't mind that her coat was hanging on my peg, I had no problem about sharing. And I had no problem that she had been using my desk, we could sit at it together until another was found. But then I heard the teacher adding, '. . . and her name is Janet.'

'What?'

'Her name is Janet.'

This was not one bit all right. It had never occurred to me there might be another person in the world called Janet. Janet was me. No one else. This girl was an imposter. A usurper. She had come while I was away sick and was trying to replace me. Trying to be me! Then who would I be? Nobody! I hurled myself at her and snatched her coat off my peg. 'You can't put your things there – it's my peg. Look, it says Janet on it, and I'm Janet.'

'So am I'.' she said.

'You can't be.'

'I am. I'm just as much Janet as you are.'

I was speechless for a moment. 'Well, you can't put your things on my peg.'

'I was told to,' she said, reasonably enough.

'I don't care. You can't. It's mine!'

She picked up her coat and put it back. 'I was told to,' she repeated stubbornly, as if that solved everything.

I snatched it off again and she put it back. The teacher paid no attention; we weren't actually hitting each other, so she left us alone.

We went on all day, snatching and shoving at the coat, during breaks and the lunch rest hour. Several children joined in, took sides, gave opinions and then got bored and drifted off. Somehow I rather liked her stubbornness, the way she stood up for herself. The aggressiveness had gone, we seemed to be going on with our feud just for the sake of it. Eventually we started to laugh. Then we laughed some more, the whole thing having lost any importance. After all, what was wrong with there being two Janets? In fact we stayed friends through all the school years, spent a lot of time together and were often referred as 'the two Janets'.

My identity crisis put to rest, school continued as a pleasant extra, something on the periphery of my 'real' life, my home life which – quiet, uneventful and satisfying – was soon to become a lot more exciting. In the meantime one of my favourite occupations was to lie under the grand piano, colouring my pictures, while my father played away overhead: Bach, Beethoven, Chopin, Scarlatti, Mozart, Liszt, Byrd – a wide variety generally. Glancing up now and then from my efforts, I could see his big shoes pressing up and down on the pedals.

I was not the only one to enjoy my father's music; the house we had bought had been empty for some time before we moved in, and rats had come to live in the garden. We discovered this because every time my father played the piano, they would come up to the house and sit in a line outside the drawing room window. We used to peer out to see them and laugh, because they looked so contented, sitting there as if they were at a concert. But they were vermin and had to be got rid of somehow. My father had the unpleasant task of catching them one by one – luring them with cheese into a wire cage and then chloroforming them – the least painful death he could think up for them. It was only when they no longer came to listen to his playing that he considered them all rounded up and caught. He said it had been hard to have to kill creatures that liked listening to Bach.

Old Neighbours; Hushed Voices

Now that Nanny Brockbank had been gone some time, and my father's new regime (his theory of child-rearing which he called 'healthy neglect') had begun, a new freedom had come into our lives.

By healthy neglect he meant that all the important things – good food, healthcare and cleanliness – should be routine, but for the rest he believed in leaving us more or less to our own devices. It was as though we knew he was watching over us from a distance, there if you wanted him, not if you didn't. And he was hard on himself, suppressing his own fears for us. He would walk away rather than call out, 'Don't do that, you might hurt yourself.'

He was, however, strict on good manners. We were not allowed to interrupt if another person was talking, and he expected us to behave like reasonable people. Other than that he did his own thing – reading, gardening and playing the piano, the sort of thing that fathers did, and left us to do ours.

Our side of the river, Bridgetown, was known as a residential area, and some of the houses, a little further from us, were enormous Victorian constructions, secreted away in vast gardens, hidden from view by high walls and trees. None of them had children in them. The occupants seemed without exception to be elderly: frail couples or maiden ladies with equally elderly maid servants or gardeners. No one you could describe as robust ever issued forth from the imposing gates of these residences.

What it had been like in the years before the war was hard to guess. Perhaps there were young parents then, and fun and laughter within those high walls, and perhaps the gardens had teemed with energetic children of all ages. If that were the case, where had they all gone? Were the fathers away fighting the war? Were the mothers doing war work and the children in boarding schools? If so, why didn't they come back in the holidays? It was a mystery to us, and disappointing because all that unexplored territory – which could have been a glorious happy hunting ground for children – was instead occupied by old people with hushed voices whom one rarely got a glimpse of, for, with all private cars being out of use, they did not even venture out for afternoon drives. Only delivery vans passed through their gates, and ancient servants making their way on foot to church on Sundays.

Fortunately though, there were children around like us, living in homes lesser than these palaces. We thought of them as palaces because of all their turrets and towers. My father called them monstrosities. Anyway, by now I had a few friends (and my sister had some older friends) to hang about with, who had much the same ambitions and aspirations for adventure as myself. We longed to explore the depths of these as yet unplumbed demesnes.

I couldn't say we devised our plan, rather it just came about, happened on the spur of the moment, a sudden impulse. We were standing by the boundary hedge of one of these gardens, one girl holding her black and white cat. Without warning, it jumped from her arms and disappeared through a gap in the fence. 'Come back! Come back, Sally!' we called, but to no avail. Sally was enjoying herself; she seemed to be sniffing the air of her new adventure as she stalked off to investigate a rose garden and then vanished from view into a rhubarb patch. Enviously we stared after her and then at each other. Then a spark entered our minds simultaneously. 'Let's go and knock at the door and ask if we can get our cat back!'

It was a great success. The maid fetched the mistress and the old lady was enchanted. 'Of course you may look for your cat. And when you have found her, come back to the house, for I think Alice has just been baking a cake!'

The morning was ours! We walked around exploring everything: lawns, trees, flowerbeds, potting sheds, disused stables, an over-grown tennis court, fruit bushes, an orchard and a walled-in vegetable garden. Every so often we called out, 'Sally! Sally, where are you?' And when we saw the gardener, a bent old man, tying up some raspberry canes, we went over to him and explained we had permission to look for our cat (so that he wouldn't get the wrong idea and chase us out). He gave us some raspberries to eat and then pointed down the garden. 'Is she black and white? I think you'll find her along there'. We raced off shouting, 'Sally!' in such a way we hoped might frighten her to run off but, annoyingly, she came up to us. Go away!' we hissed, pretending we hadn't found her, praying the gardener: wouldn't see us hurrying away and her following us.

Later, on our best behaviour, sitting upright in the drawing room of the big house and eating cake, we smiled politely as the old lady called her husband in to meet us.

'Edward,' she said, as a tall white-haired gentleman pottered through the door, holding a newspaper, 'these children were just looking for their cat in our garden. Isn't it a pleasure to see young faces around?'

'Indeed it is,' he agreed, and smiled kindly. 'And you certainly picked the right morning, for Alice only bakes once a week now.'

'It's the eggs and butter,' the lady explained, as if children wouldn't know about such things, '...hard to get.'

We nodded wisely and swung our legs, feeling relaxed now. 'Where's your cat?' the white-haired gentleman asked us. 'Did you find it?'

'Yes. We put her outside the gate and told her to wait for us. She's ever so good normally.'

'Well, do come back, whenever you like,' the old lady said. 'You don't have to have lost your cat, now that you know us.' Her eyes were amused, perhaps she had guessed. 'We'll always be very pleased to see you.'

Little by little we did all the big houses and gardens after that. It filled a need in us children, both to explore the gardens and also to get to know, make friends with, our neighbours. Even if they were old, we didn't mind, we liked them. And undoubtedly it gave pleasure to them, existing as they did in genteel isolation, probably living in terror of those telegrams that were arriving all over Britain, notifying relatives of those killed in the war – sons, grandsons, nephews.

They weren't all pleased to see us though. One old woman, painfully ugly and stooped over with a terrible humped back, chased us with a stick and called us 'little pests.' But, as we said among ourselves, it wouldn't be easy to be kind when you have such an awful disfigurement. So we took care not to annoy her again.

Suddenly there was a new word on everybody's lips. You heard it all around. People were saying: 'Have you seen the evacuees?' Or 'Is it true the Hartley's have got two evacuees?' and, 'Well, the Parkers definitely have one, I saw them with it.'

What on earth were evacuees?

They turned out to be children. Children without their parents, who had come to be safe in the country, away from the bombs of London, or other big cities. Families around and about were taking them in, giving them a temporary home until the war was over and they could go back to their own mothers and fathers. We were delighted that now there were more children in the area, but when we got to know them, disappointingly, they didn't seem much fun. Of course we hadn't the knowledge or insight to know how deeply they were suffering. All we were aware of was gloomy faces and complaints about the country being boring, and why did cows walk in the roads and leave their smelly dung all over the place? They had strange-sounding voices too – at first it was difficult to understand what they were saying, and they found us equally unintelligible. 'Why can't you speak proper?' They'd say. And we'd reply crossly, 'Why can't you?' But the will for friendship was there, and soon overcame such petty problems. In time we were going around in a firmly knit little gang, laughing at the same jokes, no trouble with communication.

Albert and Bernard were the evacuees nearest to us. They lived in a street called Jubilee Road, in a house with a green garden gate. Suitable, I thought, because the couple that had taken them in were a Mr and Mrs Greene, and I wondered if they had painted it that colour on purpose. They had no children of their own, and never invited any of us in, and as Albert and Bernard never said anything about them, good or bad, they remained an unknown quantity. I never had the feeling the boys were having any sort of family life there – simply they went in and came out of the green garden gate. But they didn't seem to mind. Probably they had hardened themselves to accept the situation and were waiting only for the day they could return home. Sturdy, good fun – Albert with curly hair and freckles, Bernard, darker, more serious, a kind boy, I always thought of them as brothers, but they were not. There was a girl called Barbara too, who lived in another house nearby, but later her mother came and took her back. She hadn't been able to bear being parted from her child. We missed Barbara, but were glad for her. I wouldn't want to be sent away from my father, but I knew he would never allow it. Other evacuees lived down in the town. We saw less of them because of the distance, although they joined in with us from time to time, particularly at weekends and most days in the long summer holidays.

Now that we were a larger group, we started to roam further a field. The road that ran past our house was called Bourton Road, and when it got to the top of the hill and ran out of tarmac, it became Bourton Lane. Stony and uneven now, it went down cutting through steep hills on either side, past a farmyard, to long watery meadows where wild irises grew, and cuckoo pint. Here there was a stream and a stone bridge and then the lane went up the side of the next hill. This whole area became our natural playground. In the fields we made camps and lit fires. We made dough from flour and water, wound it around sticks into what were called 'dampers', cooked them over our fires and ate them with salt and butter – if butter could be found. If not we brought margarine with us instead. And we put potatoes into the hot ashes and cooked them too, and anything else we could find in our larders. We made dams in the stream and we waded under the bridge with home– made fishing nets on sticks, and jam jars – and caught newts and tadpoles and sticklebacks and minnows, always returning them to the stream at the end of the day.

Someone said to my father, noticing our cockney accents, 'You're not going to let your children go round talking like that, are you?'

'Good God, why not?' my father said, 'Thank heaven children have more sense than adults.'

On the other side of our house and garden there was a lane, and off it a gravelly road called Private-Road-No-Parking. At least that was what the sign said and everyone locally had come to use it as a name. It was a beautiful little road with a wide grass verge, and from it you could see the large red stone church and the castle on its mound. Along this road too, lived our sworn foes, the Morton-Palmers. Dr Morton-Palmer was an old man, retired, and his daughter, Miss Morton Palmer, looked as old as he did; but this, we thought, was because she was so mean. The reason for our enmity was that they had two magnificent cedar trees in their garden, and on their branches were the most perfect cones we had ever seen. They had a sort of mystical, oriental shape. We had asked, very politely, for permission to pick one or two, and been refused by Miss Morton-Palmer with a kind of hostility we weren't used to. For us that amounted to open warfare. Of course we knew we couldn't trespass in their garden, but one of the greater branches actually curved out over Private-Road-No-

Parking. This by law made it fair game. The trouble was it was very high up and we were forever thinking of schemes to get up there and pick some of the coveted cones. So far, short of bringing a ladder from our house, in the middle of the night, we had not yet come up with a solution – and continued to look up at the branches whenever we passed, and grind our teeth angrily.

Further up the road, by the house of a more congenial neighbour, Colonel Hingston, there was a grass patch that produced the best daisies for miles around. This we knew because we used to sit there and make daisy chains on summer days – our own lawns being dug up for vegetables. But now that we were older we were more interested in the wood across from the patch, because it was in the form of a steep cliff, and far below, like a grey ribbon, you could see the road for Newton Abbot and Exeter. There were narrow paths in this wood, as if made by mountain goats. Who used them except us, we couldn't imagine. It was not the sort of place grown-ups would want to explore. Unless a criminal or fugitive or German spy wanted to hide himself. For us the main attraction was a cave, or to be honest, for the others it was the main attraction. I, myself, was frightened of caves. However, I would always go some of the way down, just not to lose face. Once, though, we thought we saw someone sitting right far down, probably a tramp, and without knowing why we were so scared, we tore away in blind panic, slipping and sliding along the paths as we ran until we could jump over a hedge into Colonel Hingston's garden. He was digging his potato patch and very surprised to see us, red-faced, muddy and dishevelled, running up his path. But he took us up to his house and gave us sweets, and seemed to enjoy our story.

Colonel Hingston kept a horse called Christmas, in the yard next to ours. It was a much larger yard, shared by a number of houses, built originally for horses and carriages, now converted almost entirely into garages; Christmas, a big chestnut, was the only horse to live there and we loved visiting him. His groom, Stanley, used to show us how to keep our hands flat when we offered him grass or an apple, and we would sit on the stone wall in a sort of timeless daze and watch Stanley grooming him; never for a moment imagining what was going on in the rest of England ...or Europe...or the world.

However, wheels were moving; convoys of army vehicles, British or American, were becoming a regular sight. At the sound of the trucks and jeeps and tank carriers, everyone would turn out of their houses, into the streets to look and wave. Traffic of any sort was a rarity in these times, except for local delivery vans or the doctors' cars and the town ambulance (whose number plate was, unbelievably, BOD 1, and was never referred to as the ambulance, only as Bod One).

And if any unknown car passed through our streets it was considered almost certainly to be driven by a spy. All over Britain signposts had been taken down to thwart such spies, and people were asked not to give directions to foreigners – even if they spoke perfect English. We went one better in our war effort and would enjoy standing at the crossroads, giving wrong directions to strangers, even when unasked.

One afternoon, walking in Bourton Lane, we came across a rabbit caught in a trap, Its leg was ripped open from its efforts to pull away and get free; the wound bleeding and raw down to the bone. We ran to free it but none of us was strong enough to prise open the steel jaws.

'It won't budge.'

'Keep the rabbit still, it's making things worse by jumping around.'

'Here rabbit, try not to move. We'll help you.'

'What can we do?'

'We'll have to get help.'

'From the farm?'

'No, stupid. They'd just kill it. That's why they set the trap.'

'Who then?'

'We'll go to the main road. A car might come.'

'Cars never come.'

'Sometimes they do. It's worth a try.'

We decided that two people would stay with the rabbit and three of us would run across the fields to the road.

Panting and gasping from the run, we waited. The fact that there was no sign of traffic anywhere was only to be expected. Despite being a main road, it was not wide and there were trees on either side. On the horizon more hills and the same empty road winding out of sight.

We settled down to wait. At first it seemed we would be there for ever, but then, after a while we noticed that in the distance something was happening. Sitting in the hedge, we watched as lots of little moving dots grew larger, until finally there was no mistaking what they were – a convoy! Coming this way!

'Help!' we shouted, standing in the middle of the road and waving our arms.

The front truck of the convoy slowed down and came to a halt a few feet away from us. Two soldiers stared down in surprise. The driver lowered his window and leaned out. 'Okay guys,' he said. 'Take it easy: what's the matter? Has there been an accident?'

'Yes. Yes, there has.'

'What happened?'

'It's a rabbit!'

'A rabbit?'

'It's caught in a trap!'...and we can't open it. It's too stiff.'

'Did you say a *rabbit*?'

'Yes, and it's in terrible pain...'

The two soldiers looked stern. 'Do you kids realise that all the trucks behind us have had to stop too? Just look! You've put them all out of action. And they can't pass us because these roads are too darn narrow. And because of a *rabbit*!'

'But it's so scared, and its leg is cut open to the bone...' 'Oh please help...'

There was a long silence.

The two men looked at each other. Then they smiled. The driver shrugged and got out. 'Well,' he said, 'where is this rabbit?'

'Not far,' we said, gratefully.

They walked briskly, with us running beside them. The one that was not the driver was carrying a leather case with a red cross on it. He said, 'What d'you mean not far – we've already crossed two fields!'

We came to where the others were crouching over the exhausted creature, which had long ceased to struggle. The soldiers gently freed it and laid in on the grass. Then they took bandages from their case and a couple of sticks from the hedge, and after shaking some white powder into the wound, they bound the leg neatly with the two sticks.

'There you go,' said the driver. 'Take him home with you, and care for him. In a week you can remove the splints and bring him back here to where he belongs, and let him go. He'll be fine.'

Holding the rabbit carefully, we accompanied the soldiers back to their truck, and they told us they were Americans. We shook hands with them and thanked them repeatedly, and waved until they and all the rest of the convoy were out of sight.

Later, as we were happily bedding the rabbit in a box of straw, people in the town were talking about the American convoy which had passed through the town on its way to the coast; how they would probably be crossing to France that same night, to join the fighting on the front.

Lying in my bed, just before I went to sleep, I thought about the leather case with the red cross on it. How, when the soldiers had opened it, the inside had been so neatly arranged with clean white bandages of all sizes, bottles and tubes of ointments and powders, and lots of little scissors and instruments. Perhaps I would like to be a doctor.

The Americans are Coming!

Not long after the rabbit incident – which had concluded satisfactorily, with the rabbit hopping off into the hedge as good as new – I was sitting with a friend on our garage roof, which overlooked Bourton Road. We were collecting rotten apples to drop, not on but near, people who passed below – just to give them a bit of a shock. We thought this was desperately funny because they couldn't see us and always imagined the apples had fallen from a tree which stuck out over the road. They would go off exclaiming how lucky they were it hadn't hit them – and we would flatten ourselves against the slate roof and laugh so much that our grip would loosen and we would slide down and almost fall into the next yard. To get the apples was a feat in itself, for they were only to be found in the metal gutters where they had fallen or rolled down the garage roof and been caught. There, in the fullness of time they would grow brown and soft, while retaining their shape.

Thus engrossed, we did not at first notice the trucks and tank carriers (laden with tanks), driving one after the other up our narrow Bourton Road. When we realised what was happening, we were amazed and went to squat at the front of the roof to watch. Soldiers were sitting high up on the tanks (that were on the carriers) and when they passed us, we being roughly at the same level as them, they stared, equally surprised, and then laughed and threw us handfuls of sweets, which rolled down the roof and landed in the rotten apples which were still in the gutters – not that we minded picking them out, sweets being practically non-existent in our lives.

On and on the trucks kept coming. Where were they going? We strained our necks but could not make out whether they crested the hill and went on down Bourton Lane, or turned right to go up Jubilee Road. In fact they were doing both. Why? Because they had come to set up not one camp but two.

The whole town was agog.

'Have you heard about the Americans coming to stay?'

'Stay'. Where?'

'In tents, out in the fields. They've made two separate camps.' 'Why two?'

'One is for white soldiers, and one is for black soldiers.' 'Well, did you ever hear the likes of that!'

We went to investigate. The nearest camp was in a field off Bourton Lane. It was for white soldiers. There was a stone wall around the field, which was raised above the level of the lane, and we stood looking up, wondering if we would get into trouble if we climbed the wall to see what was going on. We were just deciding we would risk it when a soldier's head appeared over the wall and seemed surprised to see us standing below in a line, deep in thought.

'Hi kids! You look kind of serious. What's your trouble?'

'We were wondering who said you could use that field.'

'Why? Do you have some sort of claim to it?'

'It's our tobogganing field.'

'Oh, I see.' He looked understanding. 'Well, I shouldn't worry about that. I expect we'll be out of it long before winter comes around.'

'Isn't it too steep for you to camp in?'

He laughed. 'All fields in Devon seem mighty steep to me. Show me a flat one.'

We laughed too. He had a humorous face with popping eyes. 'There are some,' we assured him. 'But not many.'

'Never mind. This one will do fine. It's big, and we don't use the steepest part. Is that where you do your tobogganing?'

We told him it was, and he looked impressed. 'My, I'd say you go real fast down there.'

We started to like him. And to boast. 'Very fast – like the wind;'

'No, like lightening.'

Anxious that he should understand what it was like, we persisted, 'Sometimes we go so fast we can't stop, and then we crash into the trees at the bottom.'

'Sounds good,' the soldier said.

Another head could be seen approaching. 'Who are you talking to?' it said. 'Don't you know it's a sign of madness to talk to yourself?'

Then it looked over the wall and saw us. 'Oh, Hi kids'.'

Why do they keep saying 'high', I thought. It doesn't make sense. They are higher than we are. And kids? Kids are baby goats: but they seemed friendly.

The second soldier exchanged a few words with the first soldier and then turned back to us, 'So you toboggan here in the winter?'

Their interest was gratifying, so we began to elaborate. 'D'you know, once we used a big kitchen pan – the wide flat kind they make jam in –instead of a toboggan. And guess what? As well as going down the hill, it spun round and round too – all the way!'

We laughed uproariously, remembering, and the young men smiled politely.

'Where do you live?' they asked. 'Nearby?'

We started giving lengthy descriptions, but neither seemed to be paying attention. 'Do any of you guys have an older sister at home?'

'I do,' I said, 'she's three years older than me.'

'That's no good,' one of them said.

I felt offended. How dared they say my sister was no good?

They saw our disapproval and hastened to put this right. 'We mean, have any of you got grown-up sisters – our age – who'd like to get to know us?'

But we were losing interest. Perhaps they weren't so nice after all. What was so special about having grown-up sisters? We started to move off, but paused, feeling a bit sorry for them. They looked sort of lonely.

'We'll come back again, another day, if you like? we offered. 'We can bring you our kittens to look at.'

Black and white Sally had had kittens. Smitten, we had wrapped them in a shawl and, using a wheelbarrow as a pram, wheeled them to our house for our father to see. And we had got our way; mine, Cassa, was grey and white – and my sister's was a tabby tom which she called Sabu. Two other friends also had one each.

We kept our word and took them for the soldiers to see, and they appeared to be really pleased. After that we visited them regularly and there was no more talk about grown-up sisters. Each time we left they would always ask us to come again.

We also went to inspect the camp for black soldiers at the top of Jubilee Road. There we found another world – a world of fun such as we had never before associated with adults.

There was a high fence made of iron rungs, painted black, and we used to climb to the top and just sit there, looking in at the field of big round tents, watching the ceaseless activity. As soon as they saw us the soldiers would come up and talk and laugh and invite us into the camp. In no time they were showing us inside their tents and teaching us to play baseball; Suddenly there was a whole new world for us, just up the road from where we lived.

They all had funny names like Chuck and Buddy and Earl, and we used to tease them that they were always cleaning their teeth, walking around with toothbrushes sticking out of their mouths.

Or else they would have a sort of football in their hands which they never kept still, bouncing it up and down, throwing it suddenly to each other without warning, catching it, running with it, jumping into the air and dropping it into a net on a post. And all the while they would look so mischievous, hanging their tongues out and rolling the whites of their eyes. That's what it looked like anyway, although we came to the conclusion that no one could roll the whites, only the actual eyes. Whichever way round it was, it didn't matter – we were captivated.

Our new friends never asked us if we had older sisters. It was us they liked – we weren't second best. And they loved to make us laugh, see us enjoying ourselves. Sometimes they would climb onto the tanks, high on the carriers, and shower down sweets and chewing gum so that we were running in all directions, shouting with excitement as we picked them up. When they found we were swallowing the chewing gum they were horrified, rolling their eyes more than ever.

'Not swallow it?' we cried. 'How can you chew something and then not swallow it.?'

What were they talking about? You don't put something in your mouth if you're not going to eat it. Anyway, it was rude to spit things out.

'Ooops:' we'd say suddenly, to tease, and roll our eyes like them. 'It's gone.'

And they would pretend to scold us. 'What will your daddy say to us for letting you swallow gum:'

They liked getting to know the families around and being invited for afternoon teas (so English) or Sunday lunches. We often came across them, both when we were visiting the elderly neighbours in the big houses, or in the smaller homes too. They might be mowing lawns or fixing things that were broken, or having cups of tea and a chat – effortlessly fitting into the community, helping out in the absence of those away fighting. Without reservation the people of Totnes took to them – the general opinion being that they cheered everyone up.

The white soldiers were not so popular. Rather they were regarded with a kind of veiled enmity, for many of them had succeeded in finding girlfriends, and everywhere the townspeople looked they were affronted by the sight of GIs with the local girls – whose own boyfriends were in action at the front. Or anyway, that's the way the older people saw it, even if it were not true.

We, naturally, were unaware of all this and paid no attention to the sneering remarks going round about GIs having excessively large pay packets and endless supplies of nylon stockings (why would they want nylon stockings?) being ourselves drawn more and more to the magical Jubilee Road camp.

Of course the soldiers weren't always free to play with us. If they were otherwise occupied we would climb up and just perch quietly, like birds, on the high metal rungs of the fence and wait. We were never told to go away.

One afternoon, we were passing their field on our way to a little wood to pick violets. There was a notice in the wood saying: Trespassers Will Be Prosecuted, and I had once asked my sister what prosecuted meant. 'Having your head cut off,' she had said.

'Really?'

'Yes, really.'

'How?'

'With a guillotine.'

'What's a guillotine?'

'You know the guillotine, for paper, in the photography room. With the sharp blade.'

'One of those?'

'That's right – only bigger for people.'

Once digested, I had shared the information with my friends, and we had decided that every time we went there we should be very careful not to get caught. There should be several of us so that some could keep a watch out, while others picked the violets.

Our favourite soldiers, unfamiliar in overalls, were working on the army trucks and carriers. We waved and greeted them and were about to pass on up the road when they called, 'Wait! We've got something for you.'

From the back of a truck they pulled out a few large bits of manky-looking black rubber and held them out to us.

We surveyed them doubtfully. 'What are they?'

'Inner tubes. From the tires. They're not good enough for the carriers any more, but we've patched them up and they'll be fine for you.'

'For us?'

'For swimming. Don't you swim in that river of yours?'

We continued to look blank.

'If you want them,' they told us, 'we'll blow them up for you.'

We watched as they connected a tube to one after the other and filled them with air. Tight and firm now, they could each take three or four children sitting on them when in the water. Violets forgotten, still calling out our thanks as we went, we bore our treasure back down the hill.

Tinned Food and Powdered Eggs

For some time a woman called Miss Warren had been coming in daily to cook for us. Past the age that she might be called for war duty, she had been glad, she said, to come to us – for the work took her out of herself and gave her an interest.

But now she too had left us. Her two unmarried sisters, older than herself, had become ill, and she felt obliged to stay at home and nurse them.

There was nothing for it but that my father learn to cook. We had a pre-war Mrs Beeton's Cookery Book in the kitchen drawer, left over from days of good living and entertaining in Cambridge when my mother had been there, but this was not much help to him now as the recipes presupposed luxury ingredients. The present problem was a matter of discovering how to make even reasonably palatable meals from powdered eggs, foul-tasting margerine and endless tins of spam. Or how to make the most of the minuscule rations of meat, butter, sugar, cheese, milk and eggs. These my father divided into two, every week as he brought them from the shops, and made sure that we children got half each of everything. Once I said to him, 'Don't you like butter? Or meat? Or cheese or sugar?'

He made a face and said, 'Look, I've been eating these things all my life. It makes no difference to me whether I eat them or not.'

But we were never short of food because of all the vegetables he grew in the garden. Whatever was in season we ate: runner beans, broad beans, peas, asparagus, sprouts, cabbage, carrots, potatoes, onions, cauliflower – and from the greenhouse, tomatoes and cucumbers.

Through the week we mostly ate the tinned foods and powdered egg made into scrambled egg on toast, and then on Sundays we would eat the entire meat ration in one go. My father had mastered a really good casserole which he made for us in an earthenware pot and left to stew slowly for hours. And to give us a treat now and then, he would produce a splendid chocolate blancmange, which he made in a mould and then turned it out so that it stood up like a little castle. Its outside would be dark brown and leathery, its inside tender and milky. We thought it the height of perfection.

And of course we had fruit from the garden. As well as the rickety old trees in the orchard, we had rhubarb, gooseberries, and currants; black, red and white. My father used to give the surplus to other families, where there were young children.

At that time everyone was growing things, whatever they had space for. People whose gardens weren't big were given allotments, so at week-ends and during the light evenings everyone, whole families, would be out there together. And because there were no freezers to store the produce, it got shared around instead. It became quite a social event because as well as the work, people liked to talk, maybe ask advice, across garden hedges or allotment fences.

He was always keen, my father, that we should be fully aware of the way that the whole town was being run by women. Two of the three doctors were women, the hospital was almost entirely staffed by women, the schools too. Women were running the local businesses, the shops, driving the delivery vans – even Bod One. The reason he frequently drew our attention to this was that he didn't want us ever to believe ourselves inferior to men – a common assumption in his generation. It was only within his lifetime that women had achieved the right to vote. Knowing these attitudes were still lingering around, he was determined we shouldn't be influenced by them – rather instead that we should be proud to be women when we grew up.

The only male authoritarian figure on the town scene these days was the policeman, a morose man known as PC Happy Pearce. Even if you said good morning to him he would scowl. He preferred to be scolding people, especially children, but as everybody ran away when they saw him coming, he didn't get much opportunity – which might have accounted for his gloomy expression.

Some of the women were quite authoritarian too. As was the district nurse who came to visit me when I was in bed with earache. She had been instructed by the doctor to put a hot compress on my ear. When she arrived, she marched up the stairs to my room and burst in through the door, saying: 'Now, no nonsense, young woman! I don't want to hear a single word: I know it's hot, but you've just got to put up with it!'

Every time I opened my mouth to speak, she barked, 'What did I say? Not one word!'

After she left, my father came up. 'Everything all right?' 'She put the compress on the wrong ear.'

'Why didn't you tell her?'

'She wouldn't let me.'

'Oh my God,' he said, 'is it possible I have a daughter who can't speak up for herself.'

He found it disconcerting that I was inclined to take things so literally. He had explained once to both of us that when people played the piano they were following the written notes of the music – so it was inconsiderate to interrupt them. Better instead to stand at the door and wait until the person had come to the end of the piece, and then speak. This became the normal, accepted practice in our house. But one time, having cut my finger badly with a sharp knife, I stood as usual waiting for him to finish what he was playing – holding the cut tightly with a handkerchief so that my blood wouldn't drip on to the carpet.

'Yes?' he said, turning to me at last when he had finished – it had been quite a long piece. 'What is it?'

'I've cut my finger,' I said, and the next moment fainted on the floor.

He was appalled. 'Why didn't you tell me at once?' he demanded after-wards, when I was cleaned up and bandaged. 'You should have just walked over and told me to stop: shouted at me, to make me hear, if necessary! What would you do if the house was on fire? Wait for me to stop playing the piano?'

After Miss Warren left and he had to take new tasks upon himself, he thought it would all be very straight forward and simple. Like washing our hair. We bathed ourselves by now, but hair washing was a complicated business – soap got in our eyes and stung.

The best thing for hair was called green soap, and it was soft and jelly-like. We had to put flannels across our eyes and lean over the bath while he rubbed our soapy hair up into a lather and then poured jugfulls of water over us – which was always either scorchingly hot or too cold.

'What a fuss you make:' he said in surprise as we ooohed and aaahed.

But this was nothing until he decided to dry our hair. His mistake was to think that what was right for him would be right for us too. So with each of us after the other, he put the towel over our heads and sawed it backwards and forwards until there wasn't a drop of water left and our hair-as dry as straw. This method was good for him because his hair was short, but ours was long and he had got both heads into a dense mass of tangles. When he tried to comb it we screamed and yelled, tears running down our faces.

It was too much for him. That same day, and from then on regularly, he took us to a hairdresser in the town; a tall, stern woman with a long sharp nose, called Mrs Charles. We had to sit in separate compartments with curtains around us, and not utter a sound, even if soap went into our eyes. But we didn't mind – anything was better than the torture of our father doing our hair.

On the whole, though, he was really good at knowing what to do. When we went down with the usual childhood illnesses: measles, scarlet fever, chicken pox and the rest, he never made a fuss, but he would light a fire in the bedroom of the sick person and bring in a folding table so the others could eat their meals there too. However rotten you felt, it was nice not to be left out of what was going on. And at night, when fever was often at its highest, he would stay and read your favourite books until sleep came – all night if necessary. They were not bad times.

Butterflies Impaled

I was surprised when Albert and Bernard asked me if I had seen Mr Edmonds' butterfly collection. I hadn't. I didn't even know about it. 'He's got lots,' they told me. 'Ever so many.'

'How did you get to see them?' I asked. Mr Edmonds was a rather forbidding neighbour. They explained that they could go any time. 'He likes showing them to people. I mean, if you'd gone to all that trouble of collecting hundreds and thousands of butterflies from all over the world, you'd want people to look at them, wouldn't you?' I could see their point. I had never spoken to Mr Edmonds, but if he liked people visiting, I was on for it. We rang the bell of a large blue door and were shown into a front room by a woman in an apron who might have been his wife, but equally might have been his daughter or a maid. 'I'll tell him you're here,' she said, with almost a smile, clearly accustomed to the two boys, and went to fetch the man of the house. She came back without him. 'He says you can go along to the study. You know the way.' We went down a corridor with a high ceiling and stopped to knock at a wood panelled door. A tall man wearing a black waistcoat and trousers, a crumpled white shirt and a tie loosened and askew, opened it and told us to come in. I hardly recognised him as the man I passed sometimes in the street. 'Well, you've brought a friend this time! Good afternoon, young lady!' 'Good afternoon,' I said, and looked around the room in awe. Lining the walls were glass cases, shelves and drawers. Placed here and there on the highly polished wooden floor were low tables like trays with glass tops. In the middle of the room there was a wide mahogany desk with books and papers on it, and a curving lamp with a very bright bulb like a spotlight. Mr Edmonds had a disproportionately large nose and was wearing a green eyeshade. Still addressing me he said, 'Do you like butterflies? '

'Yes,' I said, unable to stop staring around me. Everywhere there were butterflies: every colour, every size, every shape; some with elaborate designs on their outspread wings, as if streaked with a paint brush – all with vicious-looking steel pins stuck through them. They looked awkward and unnatural, pinioned to white cards with carefully written details beside each one, and their eyes seemed to be popping out. I felt sick and wanted to get away from the room.

'Smashing, aren't they?' Albert and Bernard kept saying enthusiastically, walking about and peering in all the glass cases.

'Come here,' Mr Edmonds said to me. 'I'll show you my best ones.' Mesmerised, in the grip of horror, I followed him to a case full of creatures with huge deep-turquoise wings. They looked as if they were made of silk. All impaled on steel pins.

'These are from South America – the Amazon jungles,' he said reverently. Their faces were black and furry; their mouths gaping horribly.

I hadn't thought how it might be when Albert and Bernard asked me if I wanted to come with them. It had sounded fun, seeing butterflies; I hadn't thought they would be skewered like this. We had a buddleia bush in our garden. People called buddleias 'butterfly bushes' because all the butterflies in the area would be drawn to them. Ours always had Red Admirals, Tortoiseshells, Cabbage Whites and lots of other little blue or red or yellow butterflies fluttering around it, and that was good enough for me. They were happy and free, what more could you want? They didn't have to be bigger or better.

'Shall we go now?' I said to the two boys. 'But you've hardly seen any yet,' Mr Edmonds objected. 'Come and see these orange ones. They come from Mongolia. 'I couldn't have described the feeling of evil I had in that room: those beautiful tortured creatures, that man with his big nose and black waistcoat who looked like a wicked magician. Nor could I have described my relief when I finally escaped (only after I had been led around and made to see what was in every drawer and on every shelf) from his house and breathed in the warm summer air of the lane outside.

I raced off immediately and in at our garden gate; everything seemed good again. I picked some raspberries and then a few gooseberries and walked up to the house eating them. There was something going on around the yard so I went to see. Some men were in the apple loft over the old disused stables, my father with them. When he came out I asked him why the men were there and he explained they were builders and that he had asked them to turn the loft into a little sort of house, called a flat, for an evacuee family to come and live in. 'There are not enough places for people to come to, to bring their children away from the bombing,' he said, 'and we have all this extra space.' I went away sadly. I didn't like change, and I had always loved going into the loft for apples. We used to put all our surplus apples on wide, flat trays in the loft at the end of the summer, and eat them all the way through the winter.

Streams, Orchards, Haystacks

It was the start of the summer holidays and somehow I had not yet got into my stride. I went round looking for caterpillars but couldn't find any new ones that I hadn't seen before. Then I played with my spells (Jam jars containing coloured water and chopped up deadly-nightshade and berries) and put on my gas mask, which had a sort of trunk in the front, and pretended I'd turned myself into an elephant.

My father wasn't amused. He hated to see us in our gas masks because the reality that we might need them was ever-present. And he hated too, to be reminded that human beings could even contemplate dropping poisoned gas on children.

He could hear boys and girls out in the lane riding bikes, shouting and laughing, and he said, 'It must be hard not being able to join in. I think this holiday would be a good time for you to learn to ride the bicycle. And to swim. Would you like that?'

Would I? I beamed with pleasure.

But then he suggested that I learn to read as well, and it seemed to me this was going too far. Why learn to read? I liked him reading to me, but I didn't want to read myself.

'Oh,' I said, my face falling, 'not reading, thank you.'

'It's time now, don't you think? That school of yours doesn't seem to be teaching you anything.'

I tried to explain to my father, in a reasonable way, that I had no wish to read whatsoever. I assured him that even if I could read, I still wouldn't want to.

'Look, only half an hour, every afternoon,' he replied, equally reasonably. 'It's not much of your time out of a whole day, now that it's the holidays.'

The trouble was, I couldn't really object, because he was offering to spend much more of his time teaching me to swim and ride a bike.

When it came to swimming, teaching was perhaps not the right word. He never came into the water or showed me what to do. I learned by watching the older children, down at the narrow part of the river, called the Leat, where most children from the town swam – and by trying to imitate their movements. My father would sit patiently on the bank while I floundered around in the dark, fast-running water. I was getting to the stage where I thought I would never get the hang of it, when all at once, out of the blue, not aware of doing anything different, I just suddenly felt the confidence to take off into the middle of the Leat, dog-paddling, and from that day I couldn't imagine how it would be possible not to stay afloat. It was as though I couldn't sink now, even if I wanted to.

It was the same with bicycle riding. Confidence was what it was all about. Once you could do it, it seemed the easiest thing in the world. But it took some weeks of my father walking behind with his hand on the saddle. If I wasn't aware he had taken his hand away I could ride on alone, but as soon as I knew he wasn't holding, I would wobble and fall off. By the end of that summer holiday I could ride the bicycle, swim, even roller-skate. I could also read – and needless to say, after that I never went to bed without a book.

Some way into the autumn the evacuee family came to live in the apple loft. It was now a flat with a big central room, and my father had put down a carpet which we had brought with us from Cambridge and not used. It looked really nice. There was also a bedroom and a small kitchen and bathroom.

Our evacuees were a mother and two daughters. Susie was my sort of age and Beebah was a little round-faced girl with straight hair, a small firm mouth and black button eyes. Her real name was Deirdre.

All Susie's hair had been shaved off because of lice caught on a train, and it was still only about an inch long, When I first saw her I was certain she was a boy and it took some time to consider her a girl. She was a lot like me, I thought. She liked visiting people around the neighbourhood too, and she especially liked a straight-backed, white-haired old lady called Mrs Robinson and her companion, Wendy – who kept rabbits and guinea pigs in their garden. We used to pick handfuls of dandelion leaves and then knock on their door and offer them for their pets. They would always invite us in and give us lemonade and maybe a bun. One day they had a large bowl of cherries from friends who had grown them in a greenhouse. This was a great luxury.

'Do have some, children,' they said: 'Eat as many as you like.' We ate a few but then stopped, not out of delicacy, but because there was nowhere to put the stones.

'More!' they urged, so we ate some more. What could we do? We looked at each other questioningly, each hoping the other might have an inspiration on the matter. But no luck.

Conversation was becoming difficult.

'Go on, dears,' the ladies insisted. 'Don't be shy!' And they kept passing the bowl, from one to the other of us. We didn't like to refuse but the situation was getting steadily more embarrassing, for our mouths were packed full of stones and we couldn't speak. Our cheeks were, bulging and it was too late to think of asking what to do – the stones would burst out if we opened our mouths. By now we could only nod our heads. Unable even to thank them, we managed at last to make a getaway and fled up the lane; spitting all the stones into a hedge and yelling with laughter.

Susie was on for anything and immediately joined in with the camps and the fires down Bourton Lane; the damming of streams and fishing for newts and minnows and sticklebacks – also the robbing of orchards and sliding down haystacks and running away when farm workers came after us, shouting: 'Get away, you little varmints:'

On the lookout for excitement we sometimes attempted to get bulls to chase us. Mostly unsuccessfully. One look at us and they couldn't be bothered – we weren't worth expending energy on. But after getting chased just once I knew I would never try that game again, it hadn't been funny at all. The field was boggy and I couldn't run properly, my feet kept getting stuck in the mud and I lost my shoes. Finally I flung myself at the gate, only to find I couldn't climb it because I was stumbling so much. I had to heave myself up slowly, rung by rung, expecting any moment to be crushed or impaled on horns. In fact, luckily for me, the bull had lost interest and stopped to eat grass, and Susie, who had been running too, was lying on the ground, laughing.

Sitting up in a hay barn, where we had been hiding from an angry farmer, she said to me once, 'You're very lucky.'

'Yes, I am,' I said, I always felt I was lucky, but I was interested to know why she thought so too. 'Why?' I asked.

'Your father is such a kind man.'

I said, 'Yes, he is.' And I thought, of course he's a kind man, why wouldn't he be? For I supposed all fathers were kind like mine. Even angry farmers were probably kind, if you weren't annoying them. She told me then that whenever her father, an army man, got home on leave, her mother would tell him all the bad things she had done while he was away, and he would beat her with a leather belt. It was a world I didn't understand and I dreaded the day when her father might come.

Another time she said to me, curiously, 'What colour eyes has your father got?'

'I don't know,' I said, trying to think. 'Sometimes blue, sometimes brown'.

'Don't be stupid, people's eyes don't change.'

So I looked when I got home. His eyes were definitely a deep blue. But when I looked again later, they were brown. I asked him why and he was amused. 'They don't alter,' he said. 'It depends which side you look at me from.'

It was true. He had one blue eye and one brown eye, and that was that. When I told Susie she said at least it wasn't boring to have different coloured eyes.

Fears of Invasion

My father was an older parent than average, and because he was known to be alone, looking after two young children, he was only given minimal ARP duties. These consisted of wearing a tin hat and walking around the roads and lanes at night, but near to our house so that he could come back frequently to check on us.

Normally he made no comment on what he was doing or what he saw, unless it was to remark on the brightness of the stars or some other innocuous subject. Once though, when he came in from patrolling the hill, I thought he looked unusually gloomy and asked him why.

'They're bombing Plymouth,' he said in a tired voice, 'you can see it from the top of Bourton Road, The whole sky is red over there.'

Plymouth was twenty-five miles away.

Then recalling it was me he was talking to, he added, 'They've gone now. They won't come back.'

We children knew nothing about Plymouth; that it was an important naval port and that it was being bombed night after night. People for miles around would look in a sort of horrified awe as the night sky glowed from the flames, the beams of searchlights and constant incendiaries – and tried not to visualise the buildings they once knew, now charred, gutted, collapsed, still burning. And the German planes flying low, machine-gunning the streets as men dug for families buried in the rubble.

As it continued, fears of invasion grew. One night red flares were dropped in a ring around Totnes – encircling the whole valley. This meant that bombers would come to flatten the area. My father left his post and walked down the hill as the air raid siren started up. He brought us down to the shelter, gave us the usual sticks of barley sugar, and began to read, waiting for whatever was to come.

Nothing happened. It seems that our planes drove off the attack and although it was expected they would return another night, for some reason or other they never did.

Meanwhile, unaware of the tragedies of thousands of lives further a field – in Britain, Europe, all over – country children went on with their games, their woes and their joys, for the most part happily engrossed in their own worlds of playing and imagination.

My latest absorbing interest had become the creating of small clearings, made in hedges or bushes, where fairies who had lost their way, could stay for the night. We had been given a book, from somebody's attic, with pictures of Flower Fairies, a fairy for each flower, and I was convinced that on their journeys they might sometimes feel tired, or lost and afraid. So I made little places of refuge, lined with moss and petals, for them to find. And into these I put furniture: beds and tables and chairs, which I made from acorns and oak apples and conkers.

One day though, an older girl saw what I was doing and told me that I was wasting my time because there were no such things as fairies. I went to my father to ask him what he thought. 'Look,' he said, rather sadly, 'I really haven't the faintest idea what to say to you. It's like this – I don't know if there is a God, I don't know if there are angels, I don't know if there are ghosts, I don't know if there are fairies. There may well be beings that can't be seen, but the truth is that nobody knows, nobody – however much they think they do. Everybody has to make up their own mind about these things.'

I was satisfied with that, I felt free to believe what I wanted, and at that particular point I wanted to believe in fairies. A little later I went on to other things, but without having had my illusions sabotaged, just when I was enjoying them.

Because of the war there were no toys in the shops, so our imaginations were all important. We invented and improvised with everything and any-thing that came to hand. A favourite game, when there were enough of us, was to set up two goals in a field, divide into two sides, everyone tak-ing a stick from the hedge – and provided someone had a handkerchief, we would be occupied for timeless hours, trying to get the handkerchief away from whoever had it, onto our own sticks, and then running for goal. For me there was no better game and we would come back down the lane, panting and exhausted, and flop down in our gardens to recover.

We made our own toys, from scraps of material and household things. Wooden spoons and clothes pegs were good for dolls, you could paint faces on them. Nearly all the mothers of my friends made clothes for their children, from their own old dresses or from material bought with clothes coupons from the ration books – when available, which wasn't often. From the bits left over they made dolls' clothes. Some, kindly, made things for me too, because I hadn't got a mother, and I would be thrilled with them. There were certain things a father couldn't be expected to do.

Sometimes I felt a little sad at not having a mother, like all my friends had, and would imagine what it would be like to have the sort of mother I read about in books. I began to fantasise, creating for myself a rather romantic ideal image of a mother.

But one day the more reasonable side of me, interested in the truth of the matter, said: wait a moment; Instead of imagining some kind of perfect mother who probably doesn't exist anywhere, just think of all the mothers you know – the mothers of your friends. Are there any you would like to be your own? To live with? To be yours?

That did it: There wasn't one: In fact I got quite a fright at the mere thought, and never again did I even contemplate the subject. Thankfully I had realised I was content as I was.

And not only was I content, but at the same time it occurred to me that although my father might not be able to sew dolls or do birthday parties, he nevertheless did lots of interesting things that mothers didn't seem to do. For example, he had made himself a dark room and had jars of powders and solutions (similar to my own spells and potions) and did the most extraordinary tricks which he called photography, in big flat dishes. He would let me sit up on the table and watch as he mixed his powders with stuff in bottles. (All these things he had brought with him when we left Cambridge). Then he would put sheets of plain white paper in the dishes, pour on his liquids, turn off the light – which was orange and not very bright anyway – count loudly, turn on the light again and, as we watched, brownish pictures would appear on the white paper. And not just any old pictures, like a magic painting book, but familiar-looking pictures, many being of my sister, Ingrid, and myself, when we were babies, in the garden of our house in Cambridge. And some would be of views of Dartmoor, which my father had taken before the war, before we were born, and were of scenery, with stone bridges and the River Dart.

Sometimes, too, he would buy small paper packets of different powders and crystals from the chemist shop, and at night turn out the lights in the drawing room and throw them in the fire. Suddenly we would see brilliant coloured flames leaping up the chimney, like we were having our own firework show.

The Rich on Velvet Cushions

Everyone at school, all the children that is, were talking about the bombing raid of the previous day. It had happened around midday: first the siren, then the far off crashing sound of a bomb, possibly two close together, then the all clear siren and we had come out from under our desks and got on with whatever we had been doing.

I hadn't thought any more about it but now I caught sentences flying around that were about death. Someone had been killed. I listened in silence, trying to take it in. I had never thought that people got killed by bombs. I thought they just landed in fields or knocked buildings down. I had never asked myself why they were dropped in the first place – to what purpose. Now I was hearing excited voices, clamouring, saying the railway station had been bombed, and that after the all clear siren, people had gone to look at the damage, and found a family – not local people, a mother and a father and a little girl – all dead on the platform, covered with rubble from the walls of the fallen station building.

I listened in amazement.

Dead? I thought only animals died. Because I had seen dead animals sometimes in the country.

But people? They were going on and on about it, how the little girl had fair curly hair and her hands together As if she was praying. Praying? That was another mystery. Somehow it all sounded sad and impressive at the same time. When I got home I waited for Ingrid to come back from school. 'Do people really die?' I asked her.

'Of course they do,' she said. 'Everyone dies one day.' 'Everyone?'

'Yes, everyone.'

'Not Daddy? He won't die?'

'Yes he will. Everyone will. You too'

'Me?' That was going too far. 'But I don't want to.'

What you want has got nothing to do with it. You'll die one day, like everyone else.'

I went away from her in a kind of daze, my world thrown into disarray.

For me there was only the present. I had never thought about the future, but simply assumed that everything as I knew it would go on forever. I didn't like this new scenario at all. I found myself in front of the looking-glass in my bedroom; it was on a table and I sat down and stared at myself for a long time. Perhaps I was trying to memorise my face so if I died I would still know what I looked like. Or perhaps I felt that as long as I could see myself, I couldn't die.

I continued to sit motionless, thinking deeply, until I was called down for tea, and even then while I was eating I couldn't speak, but only stare at my father and sister, still not really believing the devastating information. Could it be true? It must be if people say so! I didn't like to mention what I had learned to my father – perhaps he didn't know. It might give him a shock. I nursed my terrible discovery for a while, and then forgot all about it.

Brought up by an agnostic father and in the agnostic environment of my school, certain things had puzzled me for some time. Like why people went into churches, what they were for, and why so many of my Totnes friends went to Sunday School each week.

'What do you do there?' I would ask, a trifle enviously. But my friends thought I was lucky not to have to go.

'Oh, we get read to by some boring old teacher, and she always looks us over to see if we are neat and our nails clean.'

'And she makes us learn things by heart.'

'What things?'

'Out of the Bible.'

I had never seen a Bible. 'What's a Bible?'

But they were arguing with each other now.

'It isn't a Bible, silly, it's a catechism book.'

'No it's not. Not where I go.'

'Anyway, we only get sent to Sunday School because our parents want to get rid of us on Sunday afternoons.'

So I never really got to the bottom of what it was all about. In my school there were other children uninformed like me, and we used to climb over a grass bank and watch people going in and out of a church. And once, when no one was around, we plucked up our courage and went inside to look for ourselves. Awed by the atmosphere, the darkness and silence and stained glass windows, we crept up the aisle, peering at everything until, startled by a clergyman in a black cassock coming towards us, we fled – and when we had got a safe distance away we burst out laughing, in relief that we hadn't got caught and scolded.

Despite the lack of any teaching on the subject, in some way, from as far back as I could remember, I always seemed to have believed in a sort of presence of goodness being around – but that was possibly because I was fortunate enough to be happy. But I didn't see what that had to do with churches. The question nagged at me. I don't know what the lure was, but I asked my father, 'Why don't we ever go to church, like other people?`

'I'm sorry,' he replied. 'You can go with your friends if you want, but not with me. Nothing would get me inside a church again:'

'What's wrong with them?' Sometimes I was quite shocked at the things my father said.

'When I was young,' he said, 'not much older than you, I was forced to go to church regularly. But I didn't mind because I liked it then. I liked it because Jesus Christ was a great teacher and I admired – and still do – all the things he taught, about doing good to other people; that everyone is equally valuable in the sight of God – and so on. (But don't forget these things had been taught by people before him too, and in other religions). Anyway, I liked it, and I believed that the people in the churches, and the clergymen as well, really believed Christ's teachings – that all people were of equal value. Then I started to notice that only the rich people were sitting on velvet cushions on the seats in the front of the church, while the poor, often barefoot in those days, were standing at the back, and that they were ignored and treated in ways that I could see were humiliating for them.'

I looked at him, puzzled. It certainly didn't sound nice.

'And when we drove in our carriage, boys the same age as myself, in rags, would run beside us in the hope of earning a penny or two, for helping with bags or parcels when we stopped. I started to see how unfair things were, and that even within the church it was the same.

'But that was the olden days, wasn't it?' I said. Nevertheless, I was beginning to feel I wasn't that keen any more, 'People have changed, haven't they?'

My father evidently thought differently. 'For me,' he said, 'it's what you are inside that matters, and what you do, not what you say or what songs you sing in a church. But if you want to, go with your friends, and during your life make up your own mind what you think.'

I was losing interest. I was glad people weren't like that any more. With ration books everyone got the same now – and no one had cars so all people had to walk or catch buses.

'It's much fairer now, isn't it?' I said, soothingly, for he seemed upset by the conversation.

'I hope so,' he answered dryly, probably not wanting to disillusion me too early in my life.

In Most Schools it's Compulsory

If, as I have mentioned, my school was not exactly a seat of learning in the conventional sense, it had on the other hand, educational value of a kind not usually taken into consideration. Initially it had been started for the children of the Elmhirsts, the founders of Dartington, and to meet the needs of families who worked locally on and around the Dartington estate: the farms, the gardens, the wool mills and weaving business, the potteries, the forestry and woodlands, the general upkeep and maintenance. But gradually, as the character and spirit of the school evolved, under the singular (to say the least) headmaster William Burnlee Curry, it little by little became known by free thinking parents, disenchanted with the usual, narrow type of schooling of the day – parents who perhaps, like my father, had suffered from that system. By the time I started there, we were a some-what random, disparate collection of children. Not that we thought so, if we thought at all about such things. Which almost certainly we did not.

At the time, of course, there were many things I didn't know about, or question, but later in my life I had not been surprised to learn that only those parents who could afford the fees, paid; while those who couldn't or would find it a hardship, were not asked to. This was never acknowledged openly, but considered purely a matter between the headmaster, Mr Curry, or Curry as we called him, and the family concerned. For him it was more important that the parents of his pupils concurred with his views and the ethos of the school.

For example, it was his request that children should not be given any money from home. Pocket-money was distributed by the school. I can still remember queuing in the classroom on Fridays and receiving my weekly amount, which was according to our ages – four pence when I was eight, four pence ha'penny when nine, and so on. This we would put in our money boxes for birthdays and Christmas or spend in the local shop on a packet of sherbet powder or a bag of potato crisps with a little twist of blue paper containing salt.

I believe it true to say we all grew up not thinking about money or about who did or did not have this or that. Certainly for myself it was the case. And never did it cross my mind that anyone could be considered superior, or better than another, for reasons of money, class (something we had never heard of) or education or race or nationality. We liked people, children or adults, for being kind or fun or firm-but-fair, or perhaps simply for having a nice smile and always being ready to listen. To me, and I think to all of us, the women who came with us on the school bus each morning to do cleaning, were just as much worthy of respect as the teachers. And Curry saw to it that we knew about their sort of work too, that it should never be something that *other* people did. From the age of twelve onwards, every morning there was an obligatory hour of 'Useful Work' before we went to our lessons. During this hour the children worked at cleaning the classrooms, the kitchens, the boarding houses, the bathroom, the toilets.

Also there was work to be done in the gardens and on the school farm. One year, the older pupils painted the entire outside of the senior school from top to bottom, watched admiringly, and not a little enviously, by us juniors as they swung daringly around on the scaffolding.

My father was not quite sure at first what he thought about all this. He told me once that he had half-complained to the headmaster: 'I didn't send my daughters to school to learn to clean lavatories!'

And Curry had given him that amused, enigmatic smile and not replied.

Before my time, a group of seniors had gone to him to ask for a swimming pool; pointing out that there was an ideal spot for it in a certain small field, surrounded by trees. His answer had been: 'You dig it, and when it is ready, I'll have it concreted and diving boards put up.'

So that's what they did, working away in all their free time, some of the teachers helping too, and from then on, summer after summer, following generations had the benefit and pleasure of a really good and large pool.

Farming was another aspect Curry made sure we all knew about. At certain times everyone was recruited to help on the school farm. You could arrive in at your classroom in the early morning – perhaps with a sinking heart, expecting a maths test – and then see written on the blackboard: potato picking all today: put on your boots and get down to the farm. Far better than boring old maths! In the fields we, (teachers too) would stand in long lines as the tractor came up and down between us, sending lumps of earth, stones and potatoes flying into the air. And we would dive around, snatching and grabbing potatoes to fill our sacks, until we were exhausted. Definitely better than maths as far as I was concerned.

And spring was a great time on the farm too – new vegetables and crops of baby lambs and calves.

Another new and vital addition to everyday life was the advent of sports of various kinds – together with the sudden and unexpected appearance on the daily scene of two new teachers: a games master and a games mistress. Boxes of equipment started arriving, containing hockey sticks, tennis rackets, footballs, cricket bats and stumps. There were even batches of special sports shirts and shorts of all sizes. We stood around enthralled as they were unpacked. Curry was there too, smiling almost apologetically. 'You know,' he said to us, 'I thought children hated sports, dreaded having to do them, because in most schools in England it's compulsory and if you are not good at it you are made to feel ashamed, inferior.

It seemed nonsensical. Why feel ashamed if you weren't good at something? You could always be good at something else.

He laughed at our faces. 'Anyway,' he went on, 'a group of seniors came to me and said they wanted to do sports, and they thought the younger children would too.'

'We do, we do' we assured him fervently, in case he changed his mind.

'So I told them, 'All right, we've got the grounds, I'll have some goal posts put up.'

The new games master was called Tom Larsen. He was Danish and had a great warm, smile. He was to take football, cricket, basket ball and gymnastics. The games mistress was a comfortably-built, friendly woman. Her name was Isabel, and she was to teach us hockey, tennis, swimming and physical exercises. It was a whole new dimension to our lives and we threw ourselves into it with gusto. And for those who weren't keen, it didn't make any difference to them. They just carried on doing their own thing. We took to our new sports teachers with enthusiasm, and gratitude too.

Both were charismatic characters and in no time they had us taught and trained and going off to play matches at other schools – sometimes transported by Curry in what we called the school bus. To beat the problem of petrol shortages, he had bought an old Rolls Royce hearse, which he fitted out with seats like a little bus, and painted light blue to dispel its former associations. He had then himself – to the mystification of everyone, including my father – converted the engine to run (albeit slowly) on sawdust instead of petrol. It became a regular manifestation around the narrow streets of Totnes, the sight of which caused some mirth among the townspeople, who would raise their eyes comically to one another, but tolerantly too. After all, everyone was trying to overcome the present difficulties and shortages one way or another. And, they reasoned, wasn't it really rather resourceful of the headmaster of that school, ingenious even, since just outside the town there was a massive sawdust dump, deposited by the Totnes Sawmills. So there was never a lack of free fuel.

Market Day

Market day in Totnes was on Thursdays. This meant instant transformation from sleepy, half-empty streets with not much going on, to a day of crowds and noise, a general air of excitement and activity.

Farmers, often on horseback, and their wives and children and dogs would suddenly be all over the place – shopping, meeting friends, dropping into pubs.

From the High Street you could hear the lowing and bleating of cattle and sheep, the grunting of pigs and the occasional whinnying of horses from the pens at the back of the town where the auctioning and wheeling and dealing went on.

And in the same way that people from the outlying areas regularly entered the town; so, particularly on summer evenings and at weekends, the townspeople continually passed through and into the countryside: groups of young boys and girls, laughing and teasing; courting couples; or families walking their dogs, picking primroses, collecting nuts or blackberries, sloes, rosehips or elderberries for jams and syrups, according to which season it was. However far you penetrated into the wilds, the fields and lanes were never lonely or forbidding places. There was invariably life and action going on; farm labourers mending hedges or ditches, or ploughing behind pairs of carthorses, or reaping and stooking corn – or whatever was the order of the day. Groups of land girls (from the Women's Land Army) worked away on the jobs they were put to, distinctive in their dark green jerseys and yellowy-brown dungarees. And everywhere, children like ourselves, skulking around with muslin fishing nets and jam jars on strings, on the look-out for adventure.

Some of the people who came for walks or to pick flowers made a real mess of things, like leaving gates open or walking through young wheat, thinking it grass. They didn't mean to do harm, they just didn't know any better. But after they had gone home the damage went on sometimes for days, cattle and sheep finding their way out of their fields and wandering off, maybe falling in ditches – or crops left flattened into the mud and rotting.

We became quite indignant on behalf of the farmers and gave up being a nuisance to them, even renounced sliding down their haystacks and jumping in their hay barns. Instead we kept an eye on things for them, mending hedges where we saw gaps an animal could squeeze through, closing gates that had been left open, running for help if we found a sheep on its back and we couldn't ourselves manage to get it onto its feet.

Encouraged by the response we met with, we asked permission to go into the sheds and watch the milking and afterwards helped to take the cows back to their field.

A local breed, Devon Reds, they were all the same colour, a dark red-brown, no markings. They looked so alike to me that I asked the cowman if he could tell them apart. He looked shocked. 'Can you tell your school friends apart?'

The apex was being allowed to help with the harvesting. It would last for days and the best part was standing high up on the hay wagon, in the firmly packed stooks, and catching new stooks as they were tossed up by men with pitchforks. Land Army women would arrange them; so that they would be steady and not slide off when the horses pulled the wagons along the lanes to the barns. We enjoyed it so much they let us stay up there, lying on the straw, shouting if it wobbled too much on the journey.

In the late afternoons there would be a break for tea under the trees. The men's wives would appear, bringing kettles and teapots and baskets with cloths over them, from which would come quantities of sandwiches and pies and cakes. Babies would be put on rugs and left to kick their legs and watch their mothers. Toddlers would play among the stubble. When the kettles had boiled and the tea been made, the men and Land Army women left their work and threw themselves down hungrily. We would stand back shyly, feeling we didn't belong, until they called us to join them – proof that we had graduated from varmints to useful helpers.

Some days, through all this familiar green countryside, on roads deserted by traffic, we rode our bikes like ducks in a row – my father out ahead, then my sister, then me falling behind, trying to keep up.

In Devon, bicycling consisted mainly of pushing your bike up one side of a hill and then freewheeling down the other side because then there wasn't the luxury of multiple gears. Our bikes were painted black all over, so the shiny chrome parts (handlebars and bells and wheel spokes) wouldn't glitter in the sunlight and be noticed. By whom? Passing aeroplanes? Spies? Jerries? Anyway, it was a wartime regulation so everybody did it.

When we went to the sea, which was about six miles away, the last hill was always the best because from the top of it you could see the whole of Torbay spread out in front of you; the wide blue expanse of water, and around the coastline the small towns and villages. Then all you had to do was get on your bike and freewheel down to the beach.

Not that that was the end of your trials. The next exercise in endurance was to clamber through the massive rolls of barbed wire, erected on all beaches to obstruct invasion. This was the greatest fear throughout the country at that time – the dreaded spectre of German troops, pouring onto our beaches, brought over by night on landing barges, tanks and all. It was agonising having to slowly make your way through these coils of wire. If you hurried you got caught on the barbs, and it would takes ages to unhook yourself. And all the time, while you were having to concentrate on getting through, the only thing you wanted, were dying for, was to run as fast as you could into the blue-green waves. From necessity we persevered. Then at last, once through, we were free.

I had no interest in the sands, the shells, the rocks and rock pools, not even in the gigantic barrage balloons – anti-aircraft, made of rubber-proofed cotton and filled with hydrogen – that floated, glistening, from long ropes. Only the sea, the boundless sea, nothing else mattered. And my father, sitting on the beach, occasionally calling out to us, 'Haven't you had enough? Aren't you cold? You've been in for hours and you're turning blue all over.'

The other long expedition we did from time to time was to the moors. We would ride our bicycles to the town station and then take them with us on the local steam train to Ashburton. Once there we were on the edge of Dartmoor, and free to ride to one or other of our many favourite places – almost certainly somewhere beside the River Dart. We would swim first and then eat our jam or marmite sandwiches. Afterwards we might lie on the river bank under the trees, or on wide, flat rocks in the river, and look up through overhanging branches at the sky overhead, until we had been warmed by the sun.

If we passed a farm on the way back, my father would more often than not vanish for a few minutes into the farmhouse and then emerge looking pleased with himself, holding a paper bag with eggs or some butter or cheese.

Then down to Ashburton, freewheeling almost all the way. Onto the train, and afterwards riding through Totnes and over the bridge, there only remained the long, last push up the hill to our house.

These marathons were okay, great in fact, as long as they didn't happen too often. The real thing was what was happening around the immediate neighbourhood.

Just lately our friends, the American soldiers, had packed up their camps and moved on to somewhere else. We were really sad about that, imagining them setting up a new camp, where they would make new friends with new children something like ourselves, and we felt hurt and a little rejected. What we didn't know was that they had left to be shipped across the channel to join the fighting in Europe. They crossed to France on D day, June 6 1944. They had warned us of their coming departure, and on that day we, and a number of townspeople, had stood out in the roads and waved until they were out of sight; the black soldiers and the white soldiers, all gone, their fields empty.

Before they left, a group of us (mostly my sister's friends, but they had allowed me into their gang because there was another younger brother in it) had been collecting used petrol-drums. Every time we passed either of the camps we would see if the soldiers had more for us. We were also collecting planks and ropes. All this was for a raft we were planning to make, and before the soldiers left we had stockpiled enough empty drums to get started. We assembled everything we needed in the yard – the drums, the ropes and planks and an odd selection of nails and hammers. The first thing was to bind all the drums together to make a buoyant, unsinkable base on which to fasten our wooden planks. For days we worked on our raft in the yard, laughing and shouting and singing, and my father, digging in the garden, became accustomed to the racket coming from that direction.

One afternoon, though, it occurred to him that the noise had ceased. He went and looked over the yard wall and saw that not only we weren't there, but the raft had gone too. He often said later, it was one of the worst moments of his life. Picking up a rope as he passed, he ran through the yard and across the fields. I saw him coming from where I sat on the raft in the middle of the river. The other children had decided that as I was the youngest and lightest I should try out the raft first, and I had been very proud to have the honour. Now, however, I was having second thoughts, as half the raft had already sunk below water level and there was a distinct possibility that more of it might follow. Also, having reached the deepest part of the river, the raft had started moving rather more quickly, and I had just been wondering what to do about it.

So without doubt, my father's appearance on the scene was timely, to say the least. He threw his rope and pulled me and the now lopsided and almost submerged raft back to the bank, while the other children watched soberly, their cherished project disintegrating in front of their eyes. He wasn't angry, only relieved and, blaming himself, explained to us that any time we wanted to try it again, we must tell him first, so that he could come too – which in view of what had just happened, seemed fair enough.

Castles and Kites

There had been a lull lately, at least as far as I was concerned, for I had been in bed, and still was, recovering from measles. Hot from, fever and mildly fractious, I had spent days thumbing through books, old favourites: the various escapades of *Baba the Elephant* and *Orlando the Marmalade Cat*. And *Ferdinand the Bull* who liked flowers and didn't want to fight in the bullring. I felt a special sympathy for this bull because being tired and listless myself, I was not in the mood for combating my own various problems. The worst of which were the rumours – which Susie brought me, like news bulletins – that my cat, Cassa, had become a notorious meat robber. She had been seen on more than one occasion streaking across people's lawns with their entire week's meat ration in her mouth. She had also been caught in the act of opening doors by jumping on handles, and undoing window catches with her paw. Her bad reputation was growing daily. Susie told me that women in the neighbourhood were becoming furious and threatening to complain to my father. And what could I do, stuck in bed? Cassa was a lithe and stealthy cat and very clever – so shouldn't people have more sense than to leave meat lying around on their kitchen tables?

I decided to keep Cassa in my room until I was up and could think of a plan. I got Susie to smuggle her up to me and together we put her (and some food to keep her happy) into my toy cupboard and settled her down. She didn't mind because she didn't realise she was going to have to stay there. After a while though, she got restless and started making noises. Our cats slept in the disused stable in the yard at night and only came into the house at seven in the morning when my father opened the front door – so she was used to her freedom.

I sat in bed gritting my teeth and trying not to listen to the fuss she was making, but then my father came in. 'What on earth's going on in your toy cupboard?' he said. I don't know why it was called a toy cupboard because I hadn't got toys in the usual sense, but I kept my oddments and mess there. He opened the door and Cassa sprang out looking like some wild jungle animal. She flew at the open window and disappeared down the branches of the wisteria which grew outside.

My father was moved; he thought I had her there because I felt lonely, immured in my bedroom all day he didn't know yet that she was the terror of the neighbourhood; that any day irate housewives and cooks, like harpies, with the policeman (the perpetually scowling Happy Pearce) might knock on our door.

The other major anxiety afflicting me just then was again a matter I should be seeing to and couldn't because of having to stay in bed. Recently a woman who had been a professional ballerina had come to live near my school. She was small with dark hair drawn back into a bun, and she walked with turned-out feet and such vitality you felt she might fly off into a pas de chat any moment, even while you were talking to her. Her dance company had closed down because of the war, but it was said she had danced at Covent Garden. Her name was Florence, which sounded very grand to me. Having found a disused dance school nearby (it had been used by the famous *Ballet Joos*) she was offering to give ballet lessons free to any local children who were interested to learn.

Suddenly ballet was all the thing and we flocked, boys and girls, to do the exercises at the bar – with heady promises of graduating to shoes with points and performances in the theatre with coloured lighting. The real carrot on the stick though, was the array of swan-lakey dresses with satin tops and puffy tulle skirts we had seen in the acting cupboard.

But for the lessons, Florence insisted we must wear short black tunics with slits up the sides, and black pants underneath. These were to be made up by the mothers. For those children whose mothers for some reason or another were unable, and for me who had not a mother, a school teacher was kindly helping us to make them in sewing classes.

But now measles had held up my project and I was worried that I would be the only one in the ballet class without a black tunic. My father, whose sewing skills were limited to threading needles and sewing on buttons, couldn't have helped me, so I didn't mention my problem, but he noticed I was looking what he called 'peaky' and resolved to get me

back out into the fresh air (his remedy for everything) as soon as possible.
Although how he could have imagined I was ever short of fresh air when
I always, under his direction, slept with windows open, summer or winter,
I never quite understood.

After fevers had reverted to normal, it was customary to spend twenty-
four hours still inside the house. The next day my father let me take our
kite to a steep field in Bourton Lane; the one where the white American
soldiers had some time ago set up their camp and then abruptly left, and
it made me feel rather sad – the way in life people come and go. But we
flew the kite and it went very high because there was a strong wind. He
had to hold the string too, in case I lost my footing and fell down the hill.
It was an old military service kite, given us by our uncle who was in the
navy, on a mine sweeper. I had the idea it was for sending military messages,
but who on earth would you send messages by way of a kite? Birds?
Aeroplanes? I imagined a man leaning out of an aeroplane and snatching
a secret note from a kite as he went by, but it wasn't very convincing.

And the day after that, to re-build my health still further, we bicycled
to Berry Pomeroy castle, three or four miles away. I always enjoyed going
there because it was a real castle – or ruin of a castle – with battlements,
broad stone staircases, a great hall with fireplaces either end, dungeons
and a wooded moat. The castle was covered in ivy, and rooks and crows
rose cawing into the sky when anyone approached the drawbridge. There
was even said to be a ghost that threw itself from the highest tower into
the moat on nights of the full moon.

Off and on Berry Pomeroy had been the seat of the Seymour family,
from possibly the time of the crusaders, and was considered a sort of sister
castle to Dartington Hall – situated two miles out of Totnes in the other
direction. One could well imagine the socializing between the two
communities; the intermarrying and no doubt joint military expeditions.
For us children, spending so much of our time around the grounds of the
Hall (and who loved stirring stories of 'olden times'), it was not difficult
to visualise in our imaginations long columns of knights with their bright
banners and standards, heading off for foreign adventures, their horses
jogging impatiently, champing at their bits, as they made their way down
the long winding Lower Drive. Or, a bedraggled crowd of them, numbers
depleted, maybe limbs too, returning with their loot. A spooky Drive,
lined with ancient trees, eerie in the half-light when mists rose from the

river and floated up through the knotted branches.

Now that I was finished with the measles and back on my feet – that 'sweet reprieve' after illness that always feels so good – my niggling worries no longer bothered me. All roads were open once more for enjoying myself – what else could one want? The gang were starting a new raft. It was to be an improved model – stronger. Future voyages were optimistically (and unrealistically) envisaged – maybe all the way down the river to Dartmouth and then out to sea. Meanwhile, in some woods near school, my friends had made a new discovery – a swing (which in fact was merely a thick rope with a knot to sit on) hanging from a tree on the edge of a quarry. All you had to do was sit on it, lift up your feet, and automatically you would fly out over the quarry, high above the whole world it seemed – oblivious of the rocks and brambles below. For a time there was nothing like it – until some teachers came across it and designated it 'out of bounds'.

Also, it being spring, there was another development. Twice a year trunks were brought down from the attic and opened. Everything would be taken out, looked at, and tried on. Even curtains were changed. It was great to rediscover our summer clothes and put all the winter stuff away in moth balls until autumn, when the reverse would happen. Exciting for me because invariably my sister would have grown out of some of her clothes and my father would say, 'I think those had better go to Janet now.'

But hard for Ingrid, because new clothes were scarce, or non-existent, in the shops. Sometimes though, material could be bought and a woman found who would make a thing or two. It was the same for all children. Wearing second or third-hand clothes was simply the norm, so no-one minded, or gave it a thought. In the same way, it was normal to have the ends of our shoes or sandals cut off, so that our toes could continue to grow unrestricted when the shoes became too small. I don't think any of us even thought about the clothes we wore or, for that matter, the fact that our houses were cold in winter. There were fireplaces in each room but we understood there was only enough coal to keep one fire going all day long, in the drawing room, so the rest of the house remained pretty icy. But we didn't dislike winter, because there was snow, tobogganing, finding sweet chestnuts in the woods and roasting them. There were games and stories around the fire in the evenings and watching birds on the bird table in the mornings. We accepted that if it was winter, it was

cold. A fact of life, and good reason why spring and summer were something to look forward to.

Victory in Europe

That same spring we were asked, my sister and I, by the mother of one of our friends, if we would like to join a group of town children that were learning old English maypole dancing. My sister said no, and I said yes, so after school on certain afternoons, my father took me to the town hall and I learned to do various different chain dances in a large circle. I had no idea then, how soon and how gloriously these would be put into practice; I only knew that sometime in May a real maypole would be put up and we children would hold coloured ribbons as we danced.

The May in question was 1945, and the day we danced the maypole was 8th May, VE Day. Victory in Europe. It sounded good, but odd in a way because I thought it was Germany we were fighting. It was all a bit confusing, but I didn't mind for I was caught up in the great wave of euphoria, which was all that mattered to me. People were saying the war was over, and I knew this was what everyone wanted; was what my father always wished for at the wishing well, and I too because I wanted what he wanted. Now he and everyone would be happy. But I heard people saying there would be crowds and dancing and bonfires all that night, down by the river – and I thought they said bomb fires, and wondered why suddenly they liked bombs, even wanted them. I had thought that the main thing about the war ending was that there would be no more bombs, and here were people saying gleefully that there would be bomb fires all night long. My friends couldn't see any sense in it either, so we paid no further attention to what was being said and gave ourselves over to the enjoyment of the day.

A towering maypole was erected on the Plains. I had never imagined it would be so huge. And from the top fluttered all these beautiful coloured ribbons. The mothers had made white dresses for us to wear (one for me too) out of old sheets and curtains. We wore coloured ribbons in our hair and the usual sandals with the toes cut out. Each of us held a ribbon from the maypole in our hand and as we danced to the music of a jubilant town band, the ribbons got woven into wonderful patterns and designs, and then unwove themselves as we did the dance in reverse. I think we children were as surprised as the people watching, and we got round after round of applause after each dance had produced its own unique results with the ribbons.

'Them little maids do be just like real angels,' I heard someone say. Afterwards, back home, we had tea as if it was just another normal day. But as dusk came on and the garden grew dewy, we stood outside and listened to the sounds of music, sudden fireworks and bursts of cheering that came up the valley to us from the town.

Then some children, friends, called in. They were with older sisters, more or less young women. 'Oh, Mr Goggins,' (people in Devon always put an s on our name) 'Aren't you coming to the dancing?'

'No,' my father said. 'I am not.'

'Can we take Ingrid and Janet with us? We'll look after them and bring them home afterwards.'

'Not into the town,' my father said, 'there's probably a lot of drinking going on there – but if you're only going to be on the hill...'

So we went with them and found the whole of Bridgetown hill packed with laughing, singing, dancing bodies; faces familiar – Mr Luscombe the huge butcher with his wife and children, Happy Pearce looking reasonably friendly for once, the dairy lady with her two daughters, the wiry old postman, the blacksmith and his son.

All the young women of the neighbourhood seemed to be there, flushed and excited, confident they would be seeing their husbands or fiancés or boyfriends and brothers soon. And children, like ants, running in and out and under people's feet, joining in the action or standing on walls, looking down on the moving sea of dancers as over and over again they went through the *Hokey Cokey, Knees up Mother Brown, Hands, Knees and Boomsadaisy* or the *Cornish Floral Dance*. The brass band could be heard from the Plains, and every so often it paraded up through Bridgetown, up the hill and then back down into the town again.

The older people – who did not dance but lined the street, watching and clapping – got tired eventually, and started to straggle home. Then the mothers and children left, and we too, returned to our house. Looking back over our shoulders we saw the hard core of revelers who would clearly be at it all night, still surging around in waves, cheering and shouting: 'Oh...Hokey, cokey, cokey...' and throwing hats and streamers into the air.

Before going up to my room I went to find my father. He was sitting in the drawing room looking very serious, not at all like the crowds I had just come from.

'Why didn't you come too?' I asked him. 'It was such fun and everyone was so happy.'

'They are the lucky ones,' he said, 'and I am glad for them. But I was thinking about the families whose fathers won't be coming home. I was thinking about the parents whose sons will never return, or whose children were killed by bombs. Ordinary people on both sides of the war. I didn't feel like celebrating.'

Lying in my bed, my window open, I could still hear the town band and occasional flares of fireworks and bursts of song or cheering. I thought of the happy, dancing people out there, and I thought of my father looking sad downstairs – and a faint realisation came to me that there were different ways of looking at the same thing. Then I thought of the talk about how there would be bombfires along by the river and felt glad that no planes had come over and dropped bombs on us that night.

After the night of celebrations and dancing on the hill I imagined that things would go on much the same as before. What other way was there, anyway? I didn't know anything else. Air raids might stop, I thought, and my father would have to think of something new to wish for at the wishing well, but other than that I didn't visualise changes. Who needed them? Wasn't it enough just to be glad the war was over?

So each new manifestation of peacetime came as a surprise. The first thing I remember was my father pulling down all the black-out curtaining and burning it with a kind of relish. Then I came back one day from school and found the car in the yard. I had got so used to it being in the garage, propped up on bricks – to preserve the tires – that I was not quite sure I was pleased to see it standing there, waiting for my father to work on it and get it back into use. For so long now I had thought of it as my toy. I used to spend whole mornings or afternoons in it with my friends and we would take turns 'driving' – steering with the wheel, trampling on the pedals, pulling at the handbrake and gear stick, and at random intervals madly squeezing the rubber hooter, honking away like nightmare drivers from hell. All this in the musty, semi-darkness of the garage, closed now for years with spiders running up and down the walls. But it was a wonderful old car, a roomy, spacious Rolls Royce (year 1927) with leather seats, a mahogany dashboard and real silk curtains, cream coloured, which rolled up and down at the touch of a silk tassel. In the back there was a folding wooden table for picnics and we used to take in supplies of apples and other fruit from the garden – raspberries or gooseberries – and bread and butter and anything else we could get our hands on, and have parties there in the car, while one person at a time 'drove'.

So now I stared at it in silence, not liking to voice my disappointment in the face of my father's evident delight. Rolls Royces were one of his passions; he loved lifting the bonnet, first one side and then the other, and cleaning and polishing every copper wire or brass screw until the entire engine shone and sparkled. He would start up the engine and let it run, and then turn to whoever was there and say: 'Listen to that. You can't hear it. It's practically silent.'

From then on, any time I couldn't find him I would go to the car and look down, and as likely as not see one or both of his long legs sticking out from underneath. And he would call out, 'Is that you? Just pass me the screwdriver, will you?'

And to look on the good side of things, having the car back in use again did mean new possibilities, new excursions – I couldn't complain. For a start it was much easier now to get to Dartmoor, so we went more often. And because we had not expended our energy in bicycling (all that pushing up hills) to get there, we could do longer walks, which we did – all around Hay Tor, Dartmeet, Post Bridge, Spichwick and many other places besides. Tea rooms began to sprout in some villages so there was the added treat of dropping in for scones with Devonshire cream and strawberry jam. Without doubt things were getting less austere.

The seaside became a big thing too now that we could go by car, taking friends too, piling the car up with buckets and spades, towels and swim-suits, sun hats, toy boats, spare clothes, picnics and first-aid creams and ointments for cuts and stings, until it was like a moving hotel. Best of all we didn't have to climb through the horrible barricades of barbed wire now that they had been removed, but just run from the car straight into the waves.

This same summer a new but ephemeral development occurred in our town, which was that several shops started making home-made ice-cream and opening what they called 'Ice-cream Parlours'. The first time I saw one we were walking back from the school bus. My father pointed and said, 'Look! Shall we go in?' It was a room with tables and chairs and you could sit down and eat your ice-cream from a dish, with strawberries too if you wanted, which of course we did. I had never eaten ice-cream before, or if I had I didn't remember it, and I thought now I had never tasted anything so good in all my life. Luckily my father liked it too so I didn't have to do much persuading for future visits – just give him a look at the right moment as we passed by.

It was only some time later that the big commercial firms like Lyons and Walls got going again (having already existed before the war, and just taking their time to get steam up) and put the home-made enterprises out of business. There were never ice-creams like that again – made from the milk of local cows, pure perfection – and the parlours vanished. They came, and by the end of the summer they had gone.

Rationing continued – ration books were still used for the next ten years – but now and then new stocks of goods would arrive in the shops. Word would go round that there were shoes in the shoe shop, or material in the haberdashery store.

One time my father, probably urged on by some woman, bought yards of a white cotton organza with small sprigs of blue and red flowers, and had a dressmaker run up dresses for us – fluffy party dresses. I thought they were gorgeous. So when I got invited to a party in the town, a family I hardly knew, I went off happily, although not quite sure how one could manage a party in such a dress. The parties I was accustomed to consisted of racing around gardens and falling out of trees in wild abandon. This was a different kind of party altogether though, and I could hardly believe my ears when I heard the Mother explaining to us children, some of the games we were to play. Awful games. The worst was called Postman's Knock. You had to knock on a door and then kiss whatever stupid boy opened it (anyone must be stupid, I thought, to play such a game) with all the girls looking on, giggling and simpering in their party dresses. It was too much to expect of any reasonable person, child or no child – my sense of dignity forbade it. I drew the mother aside and politely asked if she would telephone my father and tell him I wanted to go home.

'But you can't go home!' she said, aghast. 'The party has only just started.'
It was a difficult situation.

'I would like to, please,' I persisted.

'Nonsense!' she replied, smiling kindly, sorry for me. 'I shan't allow it.
You're just not feeling well. I'll put you to sit quietly in the study and give
you a glass of water. When you feel better you can join the party again.'

So I sat scowling in the study, shaking my head every time she looked
around the door and asked if I wanted to go back to the others. It was the
first time I had felt myself in the power of someone else and I didn't like
it.

I couldn't understand why she would not let me telephone my father
and go home, it seemed a perfectly normal request.

'I'm sorry you weren't well,' my father said in the car on the way home,
the woman having made a big palaver about it to him, referring to me as
'the poor little dear'. 'Why didn't you come home?'

'She wouldn't let me,' I said, 'and anyway, I never said I wasn't well. She
said I wasn't well.'

We drove on in silence and after a while he said, gravely, 'Yes, well,
life's like that sometimes.'

There seemed a funny side to it then, and I was able to laugh. 'It was
a bit daft,' I said, 'that's all.'

Church Bells Again

It was two years now since the war had ended. We were old enough, my father said, to help with the cooking and chores generally. We would start with the Sunday casserole, into which went our week's meat ration. He decided that he would continue cutting up the meat and onions, while my sister should peel the potatoes and I the carrots. It was a long and boring job, but it didn't seem too much to ask of us, as once it went in to the oven, we were free to play with friends for the rest of the morning. And it was always so good to come back into the house and smell the best meal of the week, and know it was ready to be eaten.

Shelling garden peas or broad beans while sitting out in the garden on a summer's morning wasn't bad either, but nobody, I used to think, grumpily, could ever pretend there was anything nice about washing up. If I ever had children, I would never make them wash up. These views I kept to myself though. It was one thing to think them but quite another to say them and expose my meanness – after all, he never complained about all the things that he did. It was beginning to dawn on me that with the new privileges of growing up, came new responsibilities and obligations.

Summer had started. It was good to wake up in my-room in the mornings to the faint but lovely smell of the wisteria outside. Some of its new branches had thrust their way through my ever-open window and had tiny buds and pale green leaves, Through another window I could see the tops of the pine trees in our garden, and beyond were the familiar fields, rounded hills; always the same even while life itself changed – slowly, imperceptibly, but nevertheless changed. Little things for example, like the sound of church bells (long silenced) peeling out from the town on

Sunday mornings, or across the fields from Berry Pomeroy. After two or three times you felt you'd been hearing them all your life.

Also our lawns, which my father had dug up to grow vegetables for the duration of the war, were back to grass again – or anyway, a healthy green fuzz which we took turns watering and rolling with a heavy metal gardens roller.

We still grew vegetables and a lot of fruit, but it was good to have somewhere grassy to play, or to lie on your back on a hot day and look up at the sky. In the town there were more things now in the shops and you continuously heard grown-ups exclaiming to each other about various finds.

From the weeks of learning maypole dances in the town hall, I had made friends with some of the town children. Until then my world had not extended further than Bridgetown, where we lived (a bit out of the town) or my school at Dartington, two miles away. Now I was pleased to find myself mixing into the life of the town as well. It seemed part of growing up to go in small groups into the milk bar on the Plains, and choose from an array of milkshakes. From the milk bar we might then go across the street to the small tobacconist shop and for a few pence scraped up between us, buy tiny amounts of snuff – which we would sniff at until we sneezed, and then laugh hilariously until our eyes ran with tears.

Through my new friends I got invited to go with them and their families to the various theatrical performances and concerts around and about. There was a kind of ebullience in the air, a need for entertainment after the long years of the war. The only cinema had been bombed to rubble in the early days of air raids. TV had not yet been heard of in these parts. The wireless gave us the hugely poplar serial: *Dick Barton – Special Agent*, and Tommy Handley's *ITMA*, and shows like *Much Binding in the Marsh*, but all within our sitting rooms. Now people wanted to go out for their entertainment; dress up and mix with other people instead of huddling in their homes. And if people wanted theatre, they must do it themselves. So they did.

I loved any kind of outing and got a great kick from seeing, among the rows of seats, familiar faces from the most diverse walks of local life. But most exciting was that the children I was with invariably had relatives performing on the stage: 'Look, that's my Uncle Bob!' or 'my Aunt Ida!'

Or very proudly: 'That's my father – isn't he good?'

These would be grown-up kinds of plays, Oscar Wilde, Somerset Maugham; comedies that drew great laughs – the reasons for which I never quite grasped, but that didn't matter. The South Devon Opera Company would do a yearly production of Gilbert and Sullivan, always rapturously received. I especially enjoyed *The Mikado*, because a near neighbour of ours, a kind lady who kept guinea pigs and rabbits, and let us visit to feed them, was one of the 'three little maids from school...'

At Christmas, amid all the sparkle and excitement of that time of year, the younger local talent would come into their own, starring in the Totnes annual pantomimes – such as *Puss in Boots* or *Cinderella*. Here, older brothers and sisters of my friends, and other faces I knew from around the town, would provide a dazzling display of singing, fishnet tights and tap dancing.

At the Dartington Barn Theatre audiences were offered a more stringent diet of plays: by Ibsen, Strindberg, Chekhov and Shakespeare, while in the old banqueting hall, with its ancient high rafters, we listened in candlelight to Bach's *B Minor Mass* or *Christmas Oratorio*, or at Easter to *Messiah*.

And again, participation was open to all who had the interest and talent. One man I remember, Dick Rushton, father of two pupils at the school and chauffeur to the fleet of cars at the Hall, was for years the star performer in all the Ibsen and Chekhov plays.

In the now restored Totnes cinema, the Walt Disney film *Pinocchio* was to be shown. News of this went around like wildfire and scores of children from all parts came to view this phenomenon; many, like myself, with no idea of what a film was. Brought by our parents, we sat and waited expectantly while someone played on a piano and a magician did tricks on the stage and made jokes – which seemed very funny until he pointed to me in the front row and predicted that I would marry a man with a ginger moustache. From the general laughter I deduced this to be the worst thing that could happen to anybody.

Nettled, I was glad when the film started and the audience was swept into the colourful celluloid world of fantasy and imagination.

Shortly after that a regular weekly afternoon film show was set up for children in the Dartington Barn Theatre. Every Tuesday, after queuing patiently, we would crowd in with our bags of fizzy lemon sherbet powder, bought from the tuck shop for the occasion, jostling to get seats in the front row.

The films were all more or less the same – black and white westerns starring Hopalong Cassidy (William Boyd) who always did the right thing and upheld good at all costs and against all odds. White-haired and past middle age, with an extraordinarily charismatic smile, he was our hero and our role model. We didn't mind that all the films were so alike for there was a set pattern that had to be adhered to, and which any alteration to or deviation from would have left us indignant. Cassidy, himself, always wore black with a large black hat, and rode on a fabulous white horse, while the villain – usually some cattle rustler or bent sheriff – was invariably ugly and rode a dark, more ordinary horse. There would be a lot of very fast galloping and dust flying up, culminating in a shoot-out between Cassidy and the villain – which had to end in the villain being shot and falling from his horse, or off the edge of a cliff, after which the audience breathed a communal sigh of relief – and Cassidy would ride away across the prairie, having first restored stolen possessions and homesteads to rightful owners, or heroines to their families. All very satisfying, these films made a deep impression on our lives, or at least they certainly did on mine.

The Circus Has Come

For children a year is a long time that seems to stretch out for ever, so when in the summer months word would go round that 'the circus has come', it was like a memory from the distant past being brought back into our lives.

We would flock after school to Borough Park to watch the tents being erected, and to try and get a glimpse of the animals in their cages. These cages had a strong and powerful smell of their own, foreign and exotic, and sometimes strange, strangled sounds would come from them that we did not recognize: a roar from a lion or the chattering of monkeys. When an elephant trumpeted our blood would momentarily run cold, and then we would set off in search of wherever the unearthly cry for help had come from. Mostly the circus workers would shout and drive us away, telling us to buy tickets and come back on Saturday – which of course we did, with our parents.

Climbing up on the rickety planks, raised in tiers for seating, we would settle down under the great tarpaulin tent and inspect the contents with satisfaction. Everything would smell the same, be the same as it had been last year: the sawdust ring, the wires and swings and ropes high in the lofty domed roof, the trailing narrow metal ladders for the trapese artists. Raucous music from a gramophone, much amplified through loudspeakers, would already be blaring and a few clowns would be shuffling and ambling around, chatting to children in the front rows or playing tricks on each other to make us laugh and get in the right mood.

The other thing we liked to do before the performance started, was to survey the audience for familiar faces. It seemed as if all the Totnes people were there, all the Dartington people, and a scattering of children and families from the outlying farms. And each year, to our surprise, when volunteers were called for – as well as we children who descended from our seats in droves – some grown-ups you would never have expected, would also go down into the ring and bounce on the trampoline or do daring things to great applause. Men like our chemist, or the lady from the sweet shop, or some of the grammar school teachers, whom you normally only saw wearing suits and ties and looking very dignified – would take off their jackets and join in, flush-faced and laughing.

Of all the different and exciting turns, for me the best was always the bare-back riding. I and my friends also persevered with huge application but no success to be tightrope walkers, stringing up ropes between trees and trying to walk across, casually and nonchalently, with the ease of the circus people. This disappointment we put down to not being able to fix our ropes tightly enough – we always had the nagging belief that if only we could get a rope to be taut and firm enough, we would become masters of the art.

Shortly after the advent of the circus, usually about a month after-wards, there would be a second summer happening that would again draw crowds to Borough Park. Once more coloured lorries would be spotted making their way through the narrow streets, but this time, instead of animal cages they would be carrying enormous constructions with gaudy paintings on them, and a confusion of seats, plaster animals, bumper cars, waltzers and metal parts which, reassembled, would emerge as the Big Wheel and the Roller Coaster. Children in the streets shouted and waved as they went by, and word got around in no time.

Borough Park, situated near the station, was large and flat with well-kept grass lawns and flower beds. There was a children's area with swings and roundabouts, a bandstand where the Totnes Brass Band played on special occasions, tennis courts which were almost always in use by figures in white – young and not so young – particularly at weekends and on summer evenings after work. There were flowering trees and shrubs, even a few palm trees – proud proof of Devon's superior climate.

Suddenly this place of quiet pleasure would be transformed, and for several days, afternoons and evenings, music would pulsate from it and drift through the town, even across the river and up to Bridgetown; having a sort of Pied Piper effect on all the children – whose parents would sigh and dip into their pockets for pennies and thru'penny bits, knowing the tide could not be stemmed and consoling themselves with the knowledge that it would only be for a few days.

It seems hard to imagine a time when no one went away for their holidays. No one I knew anyway. To us, holidays simply meant not going to school; doing one's own thing. Once I was invited to go and visit a family which had moved away from Totnes and I was horrified at the very thought. Why on earth would I want to go away just when the going was really good? I'd have to be mad! All around me were my friends and endless opportunities for enjoying ourselves that didn't have to be planned for, things that just came about spontaneously. What I liked best of all was waking up on a summer's morning with not the slightest idea of what I was going to do. I might go and look for my friends – or they might come looking for me – and then we would decide what to do. Mostly we would go off into the fields and woods or along by the river. If anyone had asked us what we had been doing, we would have laughed and replied, 'mooching around' but in fact that was about the sum of it – and yet I look back on it as a golden time. Of course now that the war was long past and we could use the car again, there would be days at the beach or walks on the moors, but these were exceptions, you wouldn't want too many of them A friend's father had a motor launch and sometimes took us for trips down the river to Dartmouth and out to sea, or we might potter around in rickety old wooden rowing boats, and take a picnic in case we got hungry, but on the whole it was the things that just happened that were the most enjoyable.

At Dartington we used to hang around the tennis courts, enviously watching the adults playing – missing the lessons we had in term time. It was not long though, before we had struck a deal with some of the regular players: if we would roll the courts for them, with the heavy iron rollers at the end of the day, they would give us coaching in return. So this became a regular part of the holidays too.

There were times I didn't want to go out at all. I liked gardening with my father and I learned to sow seeds in wooden boxes and sieve the earth to go over them. He had given me quite a large bit of the herbaceous border to be in charge of, and sometimes I would go with him in the car to a nursery garden near Newton Abbot. While he was talking with the owner and choosing things, I would walk around the rows of plants and pick out a few for myself.

I found too, that you could buy bulbs and packets of seeds in Woolworth's, at the top of Totnes High Street. This wasn't easy if you were a child by yourself, unaccompanied. The assistants behind the large flat wooden counters didn't seem to think you were of any account. One time, after selecting four crocus bulbs, I stood holding out my money in my hand (I think they cost a ha'penny each), patiently waiting to be served. I stood and I stood, but nobody noticed me, or if they did, they didn't realise I wanted to buy something. I stood on one leg and then the other. Finally, feeling I couldn't bear it any longer, and still clutching the four bulbs, I left the shop and started walking down High Street. I could have felt pleased, but I didn't. In fact as I walked I felt worse and worse until I felt obliged to turn and walk back up to the shop, go inside and take up my old position at the counter, once again holding out my money and waiting. In the end the transaction took place, but the aim of this story is to back up my father's belief that you don't have to lecture children about honesty and right and wrong: if you give them the space they need, they know it for themselves. Which is the same as Socrates' theory that virtue is not taught, but 'recollected'.

I never took part in the carnival that happened every summer (only the dancing at the end), but it was still a part of everyone's life and I can't imagine Totnes without it. Friends would come for me and we would go and stand around the streets, watching as the large floats (farm lorries, normally used for transporting cattle) covered with flowers and bedecked with streamers and decorations, would make their way through and around Bridgetown, then over the stone bridge and up Fore Street. On the floats would be sitting young women with freshly shampooed hair and lipstick, and with young men beside them – very smart, glistening with hair cream and well-being and enjoyment generally. The Totnes Brass Band on a float of their own, playing full blast, would lead the way.

We would point with great interest to people we knew, or older brothers and sisters of our friends, exclaiming: 'I know him, he works in the post office,' Or 'She's a nurse in the hospital: Or 'Look: She's the one who gives us milkshakes in the milk bar!' And we would walk around, eating ice-creams, admiring the floats until it was time for the great event: the Floral Dance. Almost everyone joined in this, even if only for a few minutes, as the long line of dancers, led of course by the ubiquitous Brass Band (they must have done shifts), would snake through the town, slowly making its way up Fore Street, but turning and twisting and actually going through some of the houses, out into their gardens and then back through neighbouring houses – the owners standing by and smiling, handing us flowers to put in our hair as we danced past. At a certain point we would stop exhausted, and make our ways home. But the diehards would continue until they dropped – or, more likely, ended up in the pubs.

Ploughmen and Horsemen

Some of the events that are especially memorable to me, were not things that happened every year, you could easily have missed them. When I heard there was to be a ploughing competition, I had no particular wish to go. I couldn't see was so extraordinary about watching people ploughing, it was something I saw all the time around the countryside. But my father wanted to go, so in the end we all went. It had already started when we got there; the Totnes road being crowded with other families also on their way to watch – walking in groups, pushing prams, pulling dogs on leads, making a day's outing of it – so we hadn't been able to walk at our usual pace.

A vast flat field had been apportioned out with ropes, giving each contestant a large bit of land to plough. Finding a good place on a bank to watch from, I propped myself against a tree and looked down at the action spread out around me. At first I was more concerned about whether it would rain. The sky was darkening and although the air was warm there was a feeling of heavy downfalls imminent. Seagulls had come inland, another omen of rain, and were swooping about or settling on the newly-turned furrows, searching for worms – then flapping upwards again as the ploughs turned and came towards them. Each ploughman had in front of his plough a pair of shire horses, matched perfectly in colour and size. There were bays, blacks, roans, grey, chestnuts; some with white socks, others with stars on their foreheads or white streaks the length of their faces – but always in twos, exactly alike. Their coats shone from hours of grooming, their manes and tails had been plaited with coloured ribbons. Polished horse-brasses adorned their proud heads, their powerful chests and massive rumps. Above each poll, between the ears, little brass bells tinkled and glittered in the steely sunlight. Backwards and forwards across the long field (into the distance and then returning so near you could almost reach out and touch them), went the great horses, guided by weathered ploughmen; confident, unhurried, generations of skill and knowledge behind them; each at their own pace, in their own rhythm. The soil fell from the blades, leaving rows of immaculately straight furrows.

When Janet and Ingrid were 9 and 12 their father bought them each a horse and from then on riding became one of Janet's passions.

In those days, having a pony did not mean you were a poncy pony-club type in expensive riding clothes – whose parents drove you and your pony around in horse boxes, so that you could pass exams and win prizes. Far from it. Then a farmer would let you keep a horse in one of his fields – even along with his cows – for only a few shillings, and a pony could always be acquired if the will was there. I remember one girl buying a pony with money she had saved up from selling eggs from hens she kept in her garden. In our town the other children who also had ponies were daughters of a small-time butcher and the local builder (in other words, people without elevated ideas of themselves), while those further afield who rode were generally sons and daughters of farmers and farm workers.

I enjoyed riding on my own with no one to talk to, just Russet's jaunty ears in front of me – feeling engulfed by the countryside. Sometimes, if I particularly liked where I was I would get off, unsaddle, and sit in a field or wood or by the river until I felt like going on again. It was good to be out all day, coming back ravenously hungry just as it started to grow dark. I could go and stay with friends and take Russet with me. I had several friends on farms, and I would ride through the countryside, with my pyjamas and toothbrush in a little bag tied to the saddle, and there would always be a spare stable or field for Russet for a few nights.

Farms were paradise places for children. We were not obliged to know anything of the slaughtering of cattle, of diseases or failed crops – only of playing in the barns and orchards; visiting the cowsheds, taking in the milky-smelling breath of the young calves as they sucked at our fingers. Other smells too, of hay and dung and slightly rancid milk in the dairy.

At one of the farms I stayed on, electricity had not yet come, and every evening the oil lamps would be lit, throwing a soft, gentle light around the rooms. When I said I liked it, my friend's mother told me dryly that I wouldn't like it if I had to clean the lamps every morning, every day of my life, as she did. Nevertheless, going upstairs with my friend at night with our lamps, sleeping in a feather bed, and being woken by the sound of ducks outside the window, demanding to be let out of their shed, was the best thing I knew.

We were closer to the farmers at that time; more bound to them, more dependent, more connected. We hadn't been separated from them as we are now, by all the methods of food storage and travel that makes their work seem unreal, remote, as we open our bags of frozen or processed food from all over the world.

The worst thing about life, I thought, was the way the unexpected could happen, out of the blue. Like at a random shake of a kaleidoscope, good could change to bad, bad to good, safe to frightening – the way it happened to us one afternoon when we were riding down a steep, stony lane, a group of us laughing and talking together, with no thought of any-thing except the pleasure of the moment. Even when some boys on bicycles came hurtling out of a farmyard, followed by barking, excited dogs, I didn't see more in it than a short-lived confusion – all the horses jumping around, trying to bolt, and then it was over. Each of us being occupied with trying to calm our ponies, I hadn't seen my sister fall. Only when I had quietened my Russet did I see her lying on the ground. I jumped down and tried to help her, but then I realised she was unconscious. A friend ran to the farm for help. An ambulance was called, my father notified and told to go to the hospital and wait. After the ambulance had left, with my friends I led her horse home. My sister was unconscious for two days, but fortunately no damage was done. She recovered slowly and was soon back to riding with the rest of us.

Then a new phenomenon happened which hit me like a thunderbolt and eclipsed all. A travelling show of Russian horsemen came to Totnes. Such a thing was unheard of: On posters around the town they were described as 'Don Cossacks', but no one seemed to know what that meant. Our father explained to us that the Don was a river in Russia, like the Dart only far bigger, vast in fact, and the lands on either side formed a whole region. Cossacks, he said, were a people: warrior like tribes famous for centuries for their soldiering and horse skills, so Don Cossacks were simply Cossacks from the River Don region or area.

When the Don Cossacks arrived, an arena was built , we clambered on to the benches, and saw that all around the arena they were lighting fires, we understood there was a reason for it being an evening performance, and wave of anticipation went around like a charge of electricity.

And not for nothing, the next moment streams of riders dressed in white tunics and trousers, came galloping in at a hair-raising speed, yelling and shouting, and started jumping through the fires, standing on their horses' backs or leaping off and swinging back up again, in rhythm with the beat of the pounding hooves. And at the same time loud Russian music started blaring through the speakers. My blood turned to fire, I felt my whole personality change, wanted nothing more in the world than to be down there, doing the same things,

Riveted, I tried to watch everything that was happening. It was impossible. Whatever you looked at, you were missing something else. Then, all at once, suddenly, just as they had come so they vanished, leaving the arena cleared, empty, the audience waiting expectantly. Then one rider came along at a quiet jog, scattered a whole lot of white handkerchiefs on the ground across the centre, and withdrew back through the exit. This was followed by an ominous pause, even the music ceased. We waited, holding our breath, until out of this elide there was a thundering hooves and all the Cossacks come galloping in, and when they got to the centre each man swung down under his horse's belly and came up the other side with a white handkerchief in his mouth. After they had passed by, there was not one handkerchief left on the ground, By then I think I had stopped breathing.

When it was all over and time to go home, I had to close my eyes so that nobody could see the tears that were behind the lids. And I believe that if those riders had told me that if I went away with them, they would teach me how to ride like that, I would have gone; left my father, my sister, my home and gone. Just as well they didn't, for I recovered soon enough and had other things to do. There is always a relief in getting back to oneself, after being swept off course.

Why Take Exams?

When the debate first started circulating about the new eleven plus exam, everyone was talking about it; in the homes, around the town. It took me an age to discover what the fuss was about, for I had never taken an exam in my life. We did odd tests from time to time but the results weren't made public, even to the rest of the class – it was simply a private matter between each of us and our teacher.

'Why take exams?' someone had asked our teacher and he had laughed and told us that for sure none of us would pass the eleven plus, but we didn't have to worry here at Dartington because it only affected children who wanted to go to the Grammar School.

'Why shouldn't anyone go to the Grammar School, if they want to?' another child asked.

'I quite agree,' the teacher had replied. And that was all we heard about it for a while.

It was Curry, our headmaster, who explained it to us in one of his customary 'talks' when he discussed current issues and anything that might be on our minds. He told us that he considered it a very bad new rule the government had brought in, to make children do exams at the age of eleven, which would determine what kind of school they could attend, and what kind of futures they would have accordingly. It was unfair and stupid, he said, to believe you could judge the potential ability or aspirations of a child at the age of eleven, because all children develop at different rates, each at their own pace. And he pointed out famous brainy people who certainly would not have passed the eleven plus exams, because they were very late developers – such as Einstein, Tolstoy and Gandhi. Others too that we had not heard of.

At that time there was a variety of schools in and around Totnes. For a private conventional type of girls' school you would need to go almost as far as Exeter, and there was a minor public school for boys out beyond the moors. These two didn't count for much in most people's eyes for in fact the local children were well catered for,

In the centre of Totnes was the highly regarded King Edward VI Grammar School for boys, which provided a classical education for pupils who hoped to go to university and into the professions. The girls' equivalent was the County School and I had several friends who went there. I was quite in awe of this school – it seemed more of a 'proper school' than Dartington because they wore uniforms and looked like children from the Enid Blyton books. Both the Grammar School and the County School had boarding accommodation for children who lived in outlying countryside and had not the transport to come in daily. Mostly they would be weekly boarders.

Then a short bus ride away in the seaside town of Paignton, there was a small but dedicated convent school, which quite a few Totnes girls attended (not that they were Catholics), and these children always spoke warmly of the happy atmosphere at their school, and used to laugh because the nuns were very keen on elocution – no Devon burr survived there! But then in those days grammar and pronunciation were taken seriously in all schools, as were manners and respect.

Another school, on the outskirts of Totnes, was the Modern Secondary. Here boys and girls would go who had no aspirations for the professional or academic life, but who aimed to leave as soon as possible to follow on with the family business, learning from parents and relatives, or to be apprenticed to tradesmen of their choice – or, in many cases, to get on with the farm work they had grown up doing, and was the only way of life they wanted. And for those who were interested to learn more about farm management, there was the Agricultural College near Newton Abbot.

Nothing is ever perfect, but still for a small country town there was at least a wide choice. And both then and for years afterwards, everyone I heard talking about the new government imposition of the eleven plus exam, one and all were against it. While children all over the country at the age of eleven were starting to have to cope with finding themselves in competition with each other, even their friends and siblings – and with new emotions of stress, humiliation and lack of self-esteem.

That we at Dartington were not subjected to these exams, I am immeasurably grateful, for we had not yet learned about competition – the pride of success or harrowing shame of failure amongst your peers. For us, we did not know about shame. If we weren't good at one thing, it didn't matter; maybe we should try harder, or maybe we were good at something else. And it was with this innocence that the time had come (we were now twelve year olds) for our class to move up in to the Senior School – probably the biggest transition in all children's lives.

A New Life

The Senior School was made up of long white-washed buildings forming a square; the classrooms and boarding houses arranged around a court-yard which was half paved and half grass. Scattered groups of pupils and teachers were sitting about, sunning themselves and cracking walnuts from a tree in the courtyard. The new term had started. And with it, for us (the new arrivals) a new life. In fact you could go further and say, more than a new life, a new world had opened up; one that hinted at all kinds of freedoms and responsibilities.

Despite the friendly atmosphere, it was a bit unnerving – although we didn't care to admit it and refused to show ourselves daunted in any way. Having been big frogs in the small pond of the Middle School, overnight we had become barely tadpoles in this busy place where all the incumbent children seemed to be at least eighteen years old, about six feet tall, and to know what they were doing and where they were going. And, all importantly, why.

Given time to settle in, to wander around and inspect the unfamiliar buildings and to stock up with supplies from the stationery cupboard, we then learned that we would no longer have a classroom and teacher of our own, but go from classroom to classroom, teacher to teacher, like vagrants. Also, that there would be very few lessons, two or three a day only, and most of our work we would be doing on our own in the library or wherever we chose.

'Curioser and curioser' as Alice would certainly have exclaimed.

We would be given fortnightly assignments of work in each subject and it was up to us where and when we did them. And to aid us in organising our lives reasonably and in such a way as suited us best, we would be issued with printed fortnightly charts, giving the designated work periods of each day in squares. These we could fill in ourselves at the end of each day, and keep in a file so that at any point we could look back and see how we were spending our time – wisely or unwisely. It was impressed upon us that the charts were in no way for the purpose of anyone monitoring us. They were our private property – and our time was our own, to make our own decisions about. And therefore, self-evidently, no need to falsify the information. If we spent the morning playing tennis, or the afternoon sitting under a tree daydreaming – or gossiping with a friend – it was nothing to be ashamed of. As far as our headmaster was concerned, all children needed space in their lives to grow and evolve and think. In which case, 'mucking about' as he called it, was seen as a perfectly honourable and legitimate occupation. So, where in your chart you might write 'history' or 'maths', you could just as well write 'M.A' for mucking about. And if you found you were having difficulties in getting your fortnightly work assignments in on schedule, it would be up to you to regulate the balance in your life between working, mucking about, doing sports, spending time in the art room or other workshops, or in the music practice rooms – or anything else. You were not, of course, expected to get this balance right immediately – it would take time and experience.

To help us in this, every pupil in the Senior School had a tutor. This could be any of the teachers or house parents or the games master or mistress. As this was our first term, one of these would be allocated to each of us, but after that, as we got to know everyone, we would have the right to choose the man or woman we felt most comfortable with. Your tutor was the person you could talk to about everything and anything, on a regular basis; and who also would pass on to you how other teachers felt you were getting on in their subjects. He or she would be your adult friend, mentor – and in the case of boarders, proxy parent – to whom, if you wished, you could show your time charts and enlist their advice of any subject that was on your mind.

As the first weeks passed and the daily routine of accustoming ourselves to this new life set in, other novel concepts were introduced to us – the ideas behind them gradually seeming less strange and more appropriate. Such as that the school was not, as we had supposed, governed by the headmaster and his supporting teachers, but by the School Council – which consisting of pupils (the 17/18 year old variety) who were elected annually by all the other pupils. The Council met regularly once a week and the sessions was open to anyone who wished to take part and express opinions or just listen. It was invariably attended by Curry – who had, although I never heard of him having to use it, the power of veto. The Council also doubled as a kind of court of law, so that if anybody felt they had been wronged by another, or treated unfairly in any way, they could bring their grievance to the meeting and have it laid bare and judgment pronounced, rather than leave it festering in their minds.

Another interesting discovery was the existence of a class called philosophy (also presided over by Curry) which involved discussing questions and issues which affected us and our lives. Also current affairs and controversial topics. We would gather on Monday mornings in the large, sunny staff common room; spread ourselves around on the easy chairs and sofas, and Curry would ask if we had anything on our minds that we would like to discuss. If we couldn't think of something, he would introduce a concept himself and question what we thought about it. 'What is courage?' he might say to us. 'What does it mean to you?' Or 'Is it important to have self-control?' Or 'Who should decide what justice is? Is 'justice' giving a person his due?' Or 'Why should I be law-abiding if I don't feel like it?'

Sometimes he would get us to talk about morality versus self-interest. 'What do you see as moral obligation? Is morality more than a means of gaining social approval? More than merely expediency? After all, why should I be good? decent? behave well to others? Why is right preferable to wrong? That is, if you think it is, and if not, why not?' And he would laugh at our furrowed faces. Whatever we had to say he would always listen with respect and interest, prompting us here and there to go a little deeper, dig around a bit, question ourselves and our reasons for believing as we did; enquire whether there were more ways than one of looking at something.

Years later, after I had left school, I remember someone saying to me, 'You don't know about Descartes, Nietzsche, Kant? You said you did philosophy at your school – but you've never even heard of Socrates!'

And me, lamely, puzzled: 'It must have been a different sort of philosophy.'

And I could imagine Curry's amused smile, conveying to me: 'It's all there, if you are interested, if you want to find out. All you have to do is pick up some books.' He had always seen the business of teachers, not to stick thoughts into the heads of pupils, but to make them think for themselves. To turn the mind's eye to the light.

Rules and regulations were minimal at our school, a fact our headmaster liked pointing out in his beginning-of-term talks with us. Those few that there were, he would go over with us – speaking with a mixture of humour and common sense – so that no one could remain in any doubt or ignorance concerning their exact content and meaning.

Other schools, he would tell us, have scores of rules; some important, some petty, but either way so many that they are regularly broken or disregarded – the only consideration in the minds of the children being how not to get caught. We, he would continue, on the other hand, have very few rules – few and easy to remember – and we expect those to be kept at all times without exception.

And he would get straight to the point: 'Being a co-ed school – one hundred children in the senior school, half boys and half girls – it is essential to understand there is to be no sexual intercourse'. While we digested this and tried to think what the word 'intercourse' meant (although it was pretty obvious) he would go on to make himself absolutely clear.

'From this you are not to get the idea that there is anything bad or wrong about sexual intercourse; far from it. It is an enriching and fulfilling part of adult life.'

Leaving this to sink in, he would then make his point. 'It is a matter of responsibility, moral responsibility. As you all know, babies can result from sexual intercourse. And while adults are in a position to welcome them, make a home for them, care for them and bring them up – children on the other hand, simply are not. It can and does happen from time to time everywhere in the world, that children have babies, but when they do, this is a tragedy.'

'First of all it is a tragedy for the baby, because instead of having proper mature parents who want it, it has instead child-parents who can't cope, and mostly don't want to cope, with the situation.'

'Then it is a tragedy for the girl who has become pregnant, because it is the end of her education and plans for the future. Now she must stay at home with her parents and care all day for her baby, when she is not ready for it, and wants to be out enjoying herself and exploring the world.'

'Finally it is a tragedy for the boy, because he is morally obliged to give up his education, and maybe plans for university, and get the first unskilled job he can, so that he can start to support his child, and the mother of his child who is taking care of it all day. And this will be his responsibility all the years until the child has grown up and can support itself.'

'So the consequences of sexual intercourse can,' he told us, 'be enormous and life-changing. And because while you are here at Dartington, you are in our care – it is our responsibility to ensure you don't bring this tragedy upon yourselves.'

After giving us time to take this in, he continued: 'and the second rule – which is 'No alcohol' – is really in conjunction with the first. Again, there is nothing bad or wrong about alcohol. Taken in moderation it can be very pleasant – but it is a fact that drinking it can lower your inhibitions, your sense of responsibility, and in this case, children might, without hardly realising it, indulge in sexual intercourse, and very much regret it afterwards – for all the reasons I have just described to you,'

Phew: This 'intercourse' business was heavy going, but there was no doubt that Curry was in dead earnest. (Although why he thought anyone would *want* to ...)

The next rules were not so high powered, but were obviously close to his heart and not to be taken lightly. We were never to go swimming, either in the pool or in the river, without first having asked a teacher or a Responsible Person (the equivalent of a prefect, who had passed the life-saving exam) to watch you.

Also, we were to be sure to notify a member of staff before leaving the school premises for some reason, such as going into Totnes or further afield.

Finally, we were at all times to respect other people's privacy – both of their person and their space. Which meant not to touch them if they asked you not to, and to leave their room immediately (each boarder had their own small room) if they so requested.

That was it really. There was no mention of rules about not stealing or bullying – a universal disgust of such things being taken for granted. Anyone who digressed would soon be put straight by peer disapproval, but I don't remember any such instance occurring.

After that he went on to speak about other things, mostly of what would be happening that term, and told us we could always come and talk to him any time we wanted.

It was good to run out into the sun after the meeting, laughing to relieve the effort of being serious for so long. And although not in the mood to discuss what had been said, there was no question but that we had taken it all in; and that there was a general feeling of respect for our headmaster, for the straightforward way he always spoke to us, his humanity and dignity.

A Gentler Time

At school the new rave was the ballroom dancing class on Tuesday evenings. This was a big thing in our lives now, so much so that Monday night became hair-washing night in preparation for the next day.

Then, sharply at 7 pm, in good anticipatory spirits, we were to be found in the Assembly Hall.

Our teachers were Isabel and Bert (Isabel was our games mistress and Bert, I think, worked in accounts). Both were superb dancers, in our eyes anyway. They would announce which dance we were learning that evening – quickstep, foxtrot, tango or whatever – and then give us a demonstration, after which we would all clap enthusiastically. Then the same record would play again and with our partners we would try to emulate what we had seen – Bert and Isabel standing in the centre of the hall, watching with hawk-like expressions. Wherever they saw a couple in difficulties, they would descend on them – Isabel taking the boy and Bert the girl – and propel them into getting it right. Then, when satisfied, they would put the pair back together, and watch approvingly as the children set off with newfound confidence, (probably looking like baby ducks learning to swim).

We all loved these Tuesday nights, the enjoyment was about as high as you could get, and naturally it over spilled into other evenings, when night after night after supper, we danced relentlessly – regardless of all the other things we should perhaps have been doing. It was a general source of amusement that every evening outside the Assembly Hall door, there were always piles and stacks of books, pencil cases, bottles of ink and blotting paper – put down hurriedly by people who had been on their way to the library to work on their fortnightly assignments; but who couldn't pass the lure of the music coming from within. Talk about the road to hell being paved with good intentions.

And we would not only dance to the records of the popular dance bands of the day (Victor Sylvester, Humphrey Lyttelton) but also to our own school jazz band – which was really good, with several teachers playing in it too. Thus we learned to swap from ballroom dancing to jiving and swing with the utmost ease.

It was as yet only three years after the end of the war, rationing and shortages were still the norm. So when we (the girls that is) realised we needed very full skirts – with tight waists and coloured petticoats – for the kind of dancing we were doing, it was clear that the only way to acquire such luxuries was to make them. A flourish of industry went into action, utilizing any materials we could lay our hands on – checked kitchen ginghams, spotted curtain muslins, bright lining fabrics – and eventually, satisfyingly, the dance floor became awhirl with flying coloured skirts.

Looking back, I can see that as young people (the word 'teenager' had not yet come to us from America) we were indeed fortunate. Luckily for us we did not have today's endless magazines, mass media, commercial adverts and TV – all combining in a vicious campaign of conspiracy to make the adolescent feel self-conscious and inadequate (therefore desperately needing to spend money to buy clothes and beauty products to make themselves feel more beautiful, more attractive, sexy, impressive, powerful, successful etc.)

Thus adolescence – nowadays dreaded as a 'difficult time', (inevitably and therefore legitimately, fraught with stress, anxiety, obsessive concern about personal appearance and an almost inquisitorial criticism of parents) for us was, I think, a gentler, easier time than it is today – in which we were a little selfish perhaps, a little too careless, but on the whole a time when we were simply intent on enjoying life and its infinite variety.

And there was so much to do.

We drifted around the school in small groups familiarising ourselves with the various workshops where we could learn book-binding, pottery, woodwork or, in the large airy art room, paint in oils or water colours. Here we were free to do as we liked, without supervision. Staff were on hand, but doing their own thing; not there to monitor or supervise, but to be available if needed. It was a time for experimenting and finding out about our inclinations and abilities, as well as the actual projects on offer.

On the far side of the school there was a row of music practice rooms – small, cell-like and soundproof – each with a piano and stool, where anyone could go and be entirely alone to practise the instrument of their choice, or maybe just spend time away from people.

Finally, it was only a short walk to the school farm and there was always a constant stream of children dropping in to visit the animals and the workers; to help out where necessary or just mooch around and draw that kind of comfort that comes from keeping close to the land.

How we fitted in things like rehearsals for our annual Shakespeare plays, or concerts, I do not know, but somehow we did. It was always a wrench to leave at the end of the day. But once home, even more of a wrench to leave and go back to school. It was all a matter of what you were engrossed in.

My patient father never complained at having to pick me up in the car every evening. I am ashamed to say I took his taxi-service completely for granted.

Supper in the school dining hall was at six o'clock and then we usually danced until about nine. That was the time the boarders of my age would go to bed, and I come home. My sister would have gone home earlier; I never saw her stay for supper or for dancing. But she and her friends were top-level seniors and had perhaps grown out of such things. We were still very much the rabble – into everything that was going, which included vast amounts of sports: hockey, basket ball, gym and tennis.

The school bedtime system was very reasonable, I thought, and was taken seriously by all the boarders. Your fixed time to be in your room for the night, was according to age. But it was also accepted by the school that there would be certain nights throughout the term when a person would need an extension of an hour or so, for something like a concert, or other activity, which might go on past their set time. To accommodate this, a sort of kitty of extra hours were allowed per term for each pupil – to be taken at their own discretion for special occasions. There would be a large chart in the house parents' rooms, where pupils would fill in the extra late-night time they used – and it was up to them not to use it all up too quickly and leave themselves short for the second half of the term – and most important, for the end of term party.

There were further customs and nuances attached to this system that

I didn't know about, seeing that it did not affect me. For example, one morning when I arrived at school I was aware of a slightly heightened atmosphere; people seemed amused, even the house parents. It transpired that some of the seniors had decided to have a secret midnight party in the woods by the gym. Secret so as not to use up late-night time on the charts. And the house parents had got wind of this and tried to catch them before they were able to get back to their rooms and escape having to fill the time into their charts. This was not allowed to be done by guess-work; the culprits had to be individually spotted by staff. So the house parents had suddenly appeared among the trees with high-powered torches. It seemed that a hilarious chase had then taken place – well worth losing late-night time for, as I could see that morning by the general feeling of high spirits.

Winter Festivities

Mr Booker was our neighbour. I could remember him from the days of the war when he used to wear a tin hat and knock on our door to tell us there was a light showing through our black-out. He had been a teacher at the Totnes Grammar School, but was retired now and spent almost all his time in his garden. His wife was an invalid (I think it was Parkinson, but no one actually said so) and didn't come out of the house any more – except on rare occasions to sit in the sun. Their only daughter had married and left home some years back.

I had never heard of pyromaniacs, but I suppose he must have been one for he had a large bonfire burning in his garden every day of the year, even when there was thick snow. Day after day, year after year it was the same story; flames leaping high, Mr Booker standing around, adding more fuel or leaning back on a garden fork to admire the blaze. Such a nice man – with an almost completely round face and a perpetual smile. At least that was how he was each time I saw him. From horseback you could see right into his garden and he would never fail to give me a cheery wave. He must have run out of wood to burn years ago, but that did not deter him one bit; he was to be seen down Bourton Lane at all times with a wheelbarrow, bringing back fallen logs or branches – which he would saw up and split with an axe – or hedge cuttings from where a farm worker might be hedging and ditching.

His other passion was roses. He had a really beautiful array which he tended and cared for with the same vigour he put into his bonfires. His house was at the immediate junction where our lane met Bourton Road, and from his garden he could hear the sound of horses' hooves and know we had left our yard and were on our way towards his house. I might be alone, or with my sister, or other times friends might have called in and a group of us on our ponies be coming up the lane together. Turning the bend into Bourton Road it was customary to see Mr Booker standing behind his gate, shovel in hand, smiling pleasantly. 'Janet,' he would say, or 'Ingrid,' and nod his head in the local way of greeting. It wasn't considered necessary to say 'Hello,' or 'Good Morning,' – just your name.

He never quite had the nerve to come down the lane into our yard and ask for manure. He knew my father was also a keen gardener and probably imagined him guarding his manure pile like Smaug in *The Hobbit* guarding his treasure. So he would stand and smile at us from behind his gate as we clattered by; waiting – biding his time, for he knew – and the timing was always perfect – that at this particular point of starting out on a ride, the ponies would, without fail, lift up their tails and relieve themselves heartily. Further on up the lane we would look back over our shoulders and see him shovelling it up and carrying it, still steaming, to his roses – so happy to have got it in its pristine condition, before a passing car could flatten it into the road.

For me it seemed perfectly logical that mucking out the stable was a daily chore of my life. Just as for mothers, if they wanted babies, they must spend time changing and washing nappies. So if you wanted a horse, you must equally spend time cleaning out its stable. One afternoon, while working away in the stable as usual, my cowboy songs blaring out on the gramophone, my father called me in to take a telephone call. It was my friend Sally, who lived some miles away in the village of Galmpton. 'Can you come to a ball this evening?'

'A ball: Of course I can't.' I'd never been to a ball. 'I'm cleaning out my stable.'

'Yes, you can. Just have a bath and wash your hair, and get over here as soon as possible.'

'Don't be mad: I haven't got a ball dress.'

'Doesn't matter. A friend of mine left her ball dress last time she stayed here. She's away at boarding school now. I phoned her and she says you can borrow it – you're about the same size.'

Two hours later, bathed and shampooed, my father drove me to Sally's house, where I was to stay the night and come back the next morning. She was waiting for me outside and we went upstairs to her room.

It really was a Cinderella sort of story. I was thinking, 'Oh God, I bet this dress is going to be awful: but then she pulled out of her cupboard the most beautiful dress I had ever seen – a classic all-white tulle, with a wide bell-like skirt to the floor. And then she handed me some white elbow length gloves, silver shoes and a little silver evening bag on a chain – to keep my handkerchief in. Her older brother was coming too and he drove us down to Dartmouth, while Sally explained we were going to the Royal Naval College, and that it was a school for boys who wanted a naval career. Aged from about fourteen to seventeen or eighteen, they were called cadets while they were there, and when they left they would be sub-lieutenants and go straight into the navy, probably onto ships.

To get to Dartmouth from Galmpton, you have to drive your car onto a ferry and cross the river. From the water, looking up at the college – all lit up now because it was evening – it seemed enormous up there on the hill, and very exciting.

Inside it was not disappointing, indeed it was like a palace, and entering the ballroom, you could not even see the far end. The funny thing was that the boys, only the same ages as our boys at school, because they were all dressed in spankingly smart naval uniforms, seemed at first sight like sophisticated young men. However, in reality they were very nice and ordinary and good fun, and we were soon flying around the vast ballroom at a great rate, to the music of a lively naval band.

In those days, the norm was segregated schools (all girls or all boys) with the result that young people socializing for the first time were often excruciatingly shy when confronted with the opposite sex. For Dartington children, on the other hand, free of this handicap and having a confidence that came of knowing all the dances, knowing that nothing would faze us – it was easy to just give ourselves up to the enjoyment of the evening.

Standing in a little group, laughing and clapping after the previous dance, some cadets told me proudly that Princess Margaret was here tonight, at the far end of the ballroom, with Lord Louis Mountbatten. Would we like to all move along a bit to see them?

I had no particular interest in royalty one way or the other, but I did feel it would be very rude to go and 'look' at anyone. As if they were specimens in a zoo. I had a strong feeling about people's right to personal privacy – and even if I pretended not to be looking, I would know very well that that's what I was doing, and it would be a sort of lie. I tried to explain that I would rather not, but I could see their puzzlement. Perhaps – horror of horrors – I was anti-establishment; luckily the band struck up again and someone asked me to dance, so off I went in relief. Later that evening I did, in fact, dance with Lord Mountbatten, randomly, in a Paul Jones; a nice, grey-haired man, tall and polite – he reminded me of my Uncle Leslie, who had also been in the navy.

Back home and out on my pony the next day, riding along by the river, it was hard to imagine the previous evening had really happened – the white tulle ball dress and the silver shoes, the great ballroom and the band, the scores of uniformed cadets. Cadets that were only boys, but a million miles from our boys at school, a different species altogether. But then our boys I had known from the age of three – we had played at chasing and putting worms down each other's backs – there was nothing romantic about our boys. These cadets now, you could see them in a more interesting light, they were of the unknown, outside world...

And the days were getting darker and shorter; Christmas was approaching. At weekends we scoured the shops with our saved-up pocket money, looking for Christmas presents for friends, searching the small lighted, decorated shops in Totnes for something to catch our eye, and though in the main there was not much of interest to be found, it was still exciting. The Fore Street was narrow and from the Plains it went steeply uphill, under the clock arch to the old guild hall, the covered butterwalk and, most importantly, to Woolworths. Here you could wander around between the flat wooden counters for as long as you liked, picking things up and putting them down, deliberating over whether a friend might prefer a bottle of 'wallflower' scent or 'Californian poppy' – both priced six-pence. Or perhaps a torch with batteries, or a packet of crayons or a pretty handkerchief. For grown-ups, a teacher or a neighbour, I might go for the more sophisticated-looking dark blue bottle inscribed 'Evening in Paris', for a shilling – or something sparkly from the jewellery counter.

My father only liked homemade presents. Hitherto I had presented him with pictures done at home with crayons; now, from the Senior School I could bring home new trophies – my efforts at pottery, oil painting, book-binding, lampshades even.

The darker evenings also meant thinking up things to do inside. In a friend's house, which was rather old and dark, with corners and cup-boards, a group of us played charades regularly. Also Murder-in-the-Dark,

Sardines, Consequences and Monopoly. We played table tennis for hours too. Her parents never took any notice of us (except to come and tell us when it was time to go home) and we never invaded their space. I don't even remember their living room, or indeed if they had one. It was almost spooky in a way, but it suited us and our games.

At the same time as we occupied ourselves with these children's pastimes, a new social world was opening around us. I think we saw it as a part of 'growing up' and we wanted to avail ourselves of whatever was going. Perhaps we liked it too, simply because it was there, it existed, and because we wanted to be like everyone else – to do what other people did. How could we know then, that 'what other people did' was a very shaky yardstick, not to be relied on at all.

As I found with the question of hunting, If you liked riding it was taken for granted that you would go hunting (or in hunting-speak, 'ride to hounds').

People said, 'But you must come hunting, everybody comes.'

My father, passionately against blood sports, never stopped us from going. Agonised, but true to his theories of child-rearing, and to his trust in us, he would only mutter, scowling, 'Well, you know what I think'. But what did he know, anyway, if he never went himself? For it was so exciting, such good fun – and after all, lots of really nice people...

Meets were mostly held outside country Inns, often many miles away. To get there we would rise early and ride through the pitch dark winter mornings until we got there. On arrival we would find our friends and make a little group, as far from the huntsmen as possible – for the worst disgrace of all was if your pony should kick out at a hound.

Waiters from the Inn would be handing around trays of hot rum punch, which (without knowing what it was; only that it was hot and cheered us up) we used to reach out for hopefully. Some of the waiters would frown and move away, but others laughed and passed full glasses up to us, taking pity on our cold, scared faces – you were always scared before it started.

There were important things to be learned about hunting, like never to refer to the huntsmen's coats as red (even though they were); you had to call them 'pink' (even though they weren't), or people would sneer at you. Also, never to say 'the' hounds – you had to say simply: 'hounds', and you had to count them in couples, not singly. So if you wanted to say five hounds, you had to say 'two and a half couple of hounds'. We all adhered to this code religiously, wanting to be among the initiated; but secretly, to myself, I had to admit it was rather stupid and affected, not the sort of thing one would expect from adults.

Nevertheless, we tried to conform and appear cool and confident. I used to feel sorry for a friend of ours, Brigid, who had a lovely powerful horse and used to look very smart in a black coat and bowler hat, but whose mother (American) used to make her bring her small brother on his beloved donkey. 'He wants to go.' her mother would tell her (as if that settled everything) without the slightest idea of what it cost Brigid in loss of face. And the raised eyebrows and disdainful expressions of the other riders were nothing compared to the fury of the Master of Hounds when the donkey would bray deafeningly and all the horses scatter and jump around in fright – treading on hounds and spilling rum punch.

But all would be forgotten the moment the horn sounded. The master and whips would lead off, riders following on their well-oated horses, clattering along narrow high-banked lanes until at last entering the fields and breaking into what was nothing other than a wild free-for-all.

Nobody who has blood rather than water in their veins could fail to feel the thrill of being with a whole lot of horses, streaming out across fields and over jumps – unless they were mature enough to stop and ask themselves why they were doing it. For myself, the sound of the horn and then the thundering of hooves was like the start of a battle. I think I would have felt the same if I were taking part in a cavalry charge; no perception of right or wrong (or even why) – simply to live for the glorious excitement of the moment.

It took me time to bring myself to the point that I was prepared to be inwardly honest and acknowledge that just because you like doing something, it doesn't make it right. I never actually saw a fox being killed (which might have speeded up the thinking process) both because the South Devon Foxhounds were not very efficient, and because I never stayed until the end. After some good galloping I would leave the field and ride home. Once the horses were tired, what more was there to stay for? And each time I left I was glad to have avoided the question of a kill. Little by little though, on the way home, usually a long ride – and other times too – I would start to think over things I had heard people discussing, and each time I felt less good about my own position. I would recall the disgust

I had felt when I heard it said how if a fox went to ground, the huntsmen would send down a fox terrier to drive it up out of its hole. And how then they would catch it in a sack as it appeared, but instead of shooting it or knocking it on the head to kill it quickly (as would be done if the exercise *really* was to kill foxes because they are a nuisance to farmers) they would give it what they called a 'sporting chance' – in other words, let it go free so that the hunt could have the fun of chasing after the terrified animal again, and the hounds the reward of tearing it to pieces.

Another thing I was told was that after 'the kill' the huntsmen would cut off the tail ('brush' as they called it) and paws, and smear warm blood on the foreheads of the youngest riders as an honour. It was called 'being blooded'. An honour? Or barbarism?

In the end I knew inside me that even if an animal had to be culled or exterminated for one reason or another – and even if you never saw a fox being terrorised or killed – it was ignoble and inexcusable to make a fun outing of such an event. This did not come as a sudden enlightenment. It took time, and deep thinking about it. It was more like something gnawing at me and refusing to go away until I would look it in the eye; look myself in the eye.

In the evenings, groups were already singing carols around the town – in the Fore Street or on the Plains – and in Bridgetown from house to house. The idea came to some of us that we would go and do our carol singing on horseback to some of the outlying farms, who had probably never had people singing outside their windows. We made some lanterns out of candles in jam jars, tied to the end of bamboo sticks, but these proved a disaster. The candles kept going out and anyway, the horses went mad as soon as we tried to carry them above their heads. In the end we gave up on that scheme and took torches instead. It wasn't as picturesque, but a lot more practical.

It was good fun riding along the lanes in the dark, practicing our carols at the tops of our voices. But in the end the whole exercise became a bit fraught because every time we got to a farm, the farm dogs would rush out and bark at us, and the horses react by clattering around, making an awful din. Then the farmer and his wife would come out to see what the commotion was about, and scold us roundly. By the time we had quietened our ponies, and the farmer his dog – and we had explained that we had come to sing to them – they weren't always in a very receptive mood.

However, some were; some indeed were really nice and stood in their front porch, listening and saying afterwards that in all their lives no one had ever come and sung Christmas carols to them, and that they would always remember it. And they sent us away with slices of cake and mince pies and kind words. So all in all, although not exactly an unqualified success, it had been good. We were glad we had done it, and even gladder to get back home, into the light and warmth again.

And from now on, everyone's minds (at school that is) were firmly fixed on the forthcoming annual Christmas party. This, we were told by the older children, was the event of the year.

Semi-formal clothes were required for this very special occasion and recently, exciting-looking parcels, wide and flat, covered with brown paper, had been arriving for the boarders from their parents.

On the appointed evening, as we gathered in the Assembly Hall, there was much mirth, for we could barely recognise each other. Particularly the boys; neat and brushed, in ties, sports jackets and flannels. We were exclaiming to each other: 'Look, that's Martin, isn't it? Over there!'

'No, never! I don't know who it is, but it's not Martin!' 'Yes, it is. He's had a hair cut.'

And then we were going up to them and saying, 'Who are you?' This to boys we'd known since kindergarten. And to us, with our freshly shampooed hair and pretty dresses, they were remarking, 'You look quite nice for a change: why can't you look like that always?'

It was a great ice-breaker. By the time we went for the traditional Christmas dinner, we were all flushed from laughing and enjoying ourselves. In the dining hall, the long tables had been covered with white cloths and decorated with holly and ivy. At each place setting there was a little card with a name on it; one for each of us and each of the teachers and guests (guests were people whose work, one way or another, was connected with the school).

I found myself seated between Wilf the grounds man – who kept the gardens and sports fields – and the school dentist. Both of whom were very kind and solicitous to me; making conversation, passing dishes and sauces (offering so that I didn't have to ask), and generally helping me to behave in an adult, civilised way – instead of the usual snatch and grab with my friends. I was grateful to them for this, and quite pleased with myself too. Looking up and down the long tables and across the room, I could see my friends coping equally well, and we would signal with covert winks and nods.

After the meal had, in a timely and leisurely way, come to an end, what was really good – and a relief after the effort of being on our best behaviour – was to leave the dining hall, find our friends, and dance the evening away. But this not exclusively; for we also danced with the teachers and guests and kept the communal and festive spirit, appropriate to the occasion.

The Outside World

Spring now. Christmas and the dark winter months receding, almost forgotten. The countryside still muddy and bare, but here and there a faint green fuzz starting to cover the hedges and the bald fields. At last a very slight warmth was making itself felt in the pale sunshine.

Despite the optimism that one feels at this time of year, a shadow had appeared in my life. Nothing bigger, not a cloud, just a shadow. But one I didn't comprehend. For in what I thought of as the 'outside world' (by which I meant the social life that went on around but had no connection with my school) someone had said to me, incredulously as if I had said I supped with the devil: 'You go to school at *Dartington; that place*? Aren't they all communists there?'

'Of course not!' I had replied, hotly. Hotly because I sensed he was being critical. In fact I didn't know what a communist was – I only deduced it must be something wrong from the way he said it.

And it was not the first time that disapproval, shock even, had been evinced by people on hearing that my school was Dartington. And I couldn't understand what was bothering them. How could I? I knew nothing of how humans react when confronted by something that does not conform to what they are accustomed to. For while established practices and conventions are usually taken for granted, not questioned – the opposite applies to those who dare to be different.

Actually, the rumour of a communist connection was quite amusing as I realised later, when it came to light; because it was simply due to the newspapers the school was ordering locally. Outside the staff common room there was a large table on which every morning a wide selection of daily papers were laid out for the use of teachers and pupils – anyone who was interested.

Curry, typically wishing to be non-biased, saw to it that these ranged from the conservative *Times* and *Telegraph*, the liberal *News Chronicle*, the Labour *Mail* and *Manchester Guardian* and the communist *Daily Worker*. But it was, of course, the latter that was singled out for special attention by the people who worked in the Totnes news agent. I don't know whether it went so far as to get up their noses and scandalise them, or whether they merely thought it mildly interesting information – but one way or the other, word went around until it became common knowledge that 'those Dartington people' were raving communists.

Utterly in the dark as to what lay behind the strange looks or shocked responses I was starting to get concerning where I went to school – it was, as it turned out, only the beginning of a long process of learning about the prejudices the 'outside world' later proved to be awash with. Most of which I was unaware of until after I left school. And then it was my turn to be shocked – to find that some people looked down on others, or believed themselves superior, for reasons of money, class, colour, race, religion, education or even material possessions. I was as yet to discover all this, and come to see (for if you have not been indoctrinated it is self-evident) that as well as being ridiculous, these values inevitably caused those afflicted with them to become greedy, selfish, acquisitive, self-important, uncaring – finally cruel and ruthless.

But now, mercifully, all this was still a long way ahead. For the time being I was intent on enjoying myself, so I tried to ignore the rather puzzling pinpricks and get on with my life.

It being spring, all sorts of new activities were on offer. The large grass courtyard at school was ideal for doing country dancing and gym outside. For gym, the mats and gymnastic apparatus were brought out and with our gym teacher, Tom Larsen, standing by, queues formed for children of all ages to run barefoot across the grass and hurtle themselves into the air. Other people who were not taking part would sit around in groups, watching. Some adults too. There was a feeling that summer was in the air, imminent. Cuckoos could be heard in the woods.

Swimming also had started. Short dips only because the water was still cold. Sitting on the grass bank beside the pool with a friend, deliberating on whether or not to run and jump in, our headmaster, Curry, walked by. Seeing us, he came over and sat down. 'Thinking of going in?'

'Just thinking about it,' we said, and laughed.

'You've taken to wearing swimsuits I see:' He was smiling.

We hung our heads, embarrassed, and muttered 'Mmmnn,' and 'Yes, sort of.'

He was a man always deeply interested in what other people thought or felt. 'You feel better like that? More comfortable with yourselves, more at ease?'

We nodded.

'Well, that's what matters, isn't it? It's a personal thing, and it's good to know what feels best for you.'

Still embarrassed, we didn't know how to explain to him that although we had always swum at school without clothes, since kindergarten – taken it for granted, felt natural about it – we were beginning to be aware that for some reason 'other people' didn't. And that therefore there must somehow be something wrong with it. We had always worn swimsuits at the beach of course, because that's what everybody there did – and that had seemed natural too. In fact the matter had seemed of so small importance, so trivial, that we had never bothered to give it any thought. Previously, that is. Now, for some reason which we would have been hard put to explain, the opinions of strangers were starting to take precedence over people we'd known all our lives; invade our ways and customs which until now we had felt perfectly happy with. We felt like traitors. I think he was trying not to laugh, but there was sympathy in his voice as he said, 'I know. Believe me, I understand.' We looked at him then and we saw that he really did understand. For he knew what lay ahead for us, for all people who were just a little bit different. And because of this, and that he was responsible for it, there was an apologetic expression on his face. He just wanted, he said, for us to feel free to make our own choices – not be hidebound by mindless rules and conventions, by authority and fear.

Singing had invariably been an important part of our lives. In the Middle School a double period every week had always been given over to a couple of hours of singing – lustily, at the tops of our voices. Anything and everything from song books containing old English folk songs, sea-faring songs, early American country songs, German Lieder of the Schumann, Schubert, Mozart variety. Always a great pleasure for us children to climb the stairs to the large, sunny music room and stand in rows, thumbing through the song books while our music teacher, Tan, played little introductory themes to get us in the mood. And then opening our lungs to the heavens and bellowing forth. The time always passed too quickly, but if you were keen you could ask for extra singing lessons during the week, on your own, singly, as I and some of my friends did. Now, in the senior school, there was a more serious attitude to music and it being the time of year coming up to Easter, we were rehearsing *Messiah*, to be sung in the great Banqueting hall of the old original Hall itself.

As well as this, because of the better weather, sports were taking off with away matches being arranged with other schools at the weekends. Although being enthusiastic, I was nevertheless not sure I liked this infringement on my time for doing my own thing at home, and even considered opting out of my positions on the teams. However, the lure was too great, especially as our games teacher, Tom Larsen, used to drive those of us in the tennis team in his roomy, dark green, open-roofed vintage Lagonda, through the countryside to vanquish our foes – or attempt to. Definitely too good to miss.

It was around this time of our first spring as seniors, that we were told 'inspectors' would be visiting us some time during the next week. Inspectors: What were they coming to inspect? And why? What had we done wrong?

All schools were visited by government inspectors, we were told. It was a good thing because it meant sub-standard schools wouldn't be allowed to continue functioning. We didn't have to do anything special, just carry on as normal, but not be surprised if unknown men or women came into our classes, or the library or dining hall, and sat for a while, watching. Also, they might want to talk to some of us, ask questions and, if so, we were to be friendly and natural, and tell them whatever they wanted to know.

So we didn't really mind seeing strangers walking around in little groups, or appearing suddenly and intermingling with us. They seemed pleasant enough people, even quite fun, and genuinely interested in what we did and what we thought.

The following day in a lesson, our history teacher, Ted Fitch, told us the inspectors had said in the staff common room that they were very favourably impressed. And that, although we were secular or agnostic – in other words we didn't do God they felt Dartington to be the most Christian in spirit of all the schools they had visited. We heard the same from other teachers too. They all seemed rather amused and quite pleased, which we found distinctly strange. If we weren't Christians, why would we want people to think we were *like* Christians?

We're Going to Miss You

Post war Britain was emerging as something almost tangible. It was evolving, starting to pulsate; it was in the process of becoming. It was a time of hope, of flux; new ways, new developments, an awareness of new opportunities.

People wanted to forget about suffering and fear and separation from loved ones. Inevitably old relationships were coming unstuck, new ones were being forged. All longed for the fruits of peacetime; for gaiety, frivolity even. And what they wanted, the shops and businesses were anxious to provide – as far as they could under the still straightened circumstances, for rationing continued to exist for many years to come. Dreams and aspirations became bound up with supply and demand. Shoppers wanted to buy luxuries that would change life-styles, transform lives.

For us children, too young to have known pre-war conditions, the word luxury meant nothing. Neither were we aware of having been through a time of deprivation. And what was 'austerity' anyway? To hear grown-ups talking, it meant powdered egg and M&V (tins of meat and vegetables) both of which we liked a lot. The fact that they were no longer available was deprivation as far as we were concerned. On the plus side though, there were now bananas, oranges, peaches and melons in the greengrocers; delights hitherto undreamed of. It was only much later that aubergines, courgettes and green peppers made an appearance in the local shops – mostly to be eyed with suspicion and left to rot.

In the cinemas American films promoted glamour, romance and easy living, which in turn were reflected in the new fashions in clothes and food, and stimulated interest in travel and holidays abroad, for those who could afford it.

It goes without saying that in those days before mass media, the post-war influences were slower in coming to places like Totnes – small towns and villages tucked away in the country, far from London and the big industrial towns. But very gradually even here hints and indications manifested themselves, pointing to what was to come.

Such as when the exciting news went around that a batch of real American denim jeans had come into some shop in Exeter (about twenty miles away) – jeans being something we only saw in films or worn by those fortunates who had relatives in America who sent them parcels of jeans and comics. It was like a bird migration, all anybody wanted was to get to Exeter somehow. I was lucky enough to be invited to go by car with a friend and her mother, and we just managed to get a pair each before stocks ran out, leaving scores of dejected, disappointed children to trail back home empty-handed. The said mother, however, considered flies indelicate on girls, so when we got home we had to wait impatiently while she got out her sewing machine and relocated the offending zips.

There was definitely a buzz to this time; those early stages of growing up when you hardly realised it. We were starting to bloom, to glow. My taste in reading changed. Zane Grey became my favourite author, because he wrote not only about adventures, as my children's books had, but of the lure of mountains, and wide flat prairies; of waving grasses and the sage in bloom. And most importantly, of the ideal of pursuing justice and assisting the weak. His titles: *Tall in the Saddle*, and *Silver on the Sage* seemed somehow thrilling and adult. My favourite song of that time was *The Call of the Far Away Hills*. I yearned for far horizons, where land met sky, to feel the whole world nothing but blue space and sunshine, everything else illusion.

Meanwhile reality, in the guise of the social world around me, was breaking in on my life. A mixed pleasure I was to find. Nevertheless I accepted invitations with interest – mostly dancing or tennis parties, held at the homes of children who went to boarding schools, their parents combing the county for young people to invite to meet them in the holidays. If the fly in the ointment was to reveal itself, it would do so early on, when opening lines of conversation were made.

'So, where do you go to school?'

And I would answer, 'Dartington. It's near Totnes.'

'Not... Dartington Hall?'

'Yes, Dartington Hall.'

'Oh I say, really? That place? I mean that place where they...? But, isn't it...?'

'Isn't it what?'

Tittering laughter. 'Well, I mean, isn't it a sort of nudist colony? Or a communist settlement? A bit weird?'

'Of course it's not: It's not at all weird.'

And because we were a co-ed school (unusual in those days) you could almost see them thinking we were probably all at it like rabbits. And it would be useless to tell them how far that was from the truth, because their minds would be made up.

I had not yet heard of the word 'discrimination' but now I was learning the meaning of it by experiencing it. I was being judged not for the colour of my skin or my class but for the school I went to. Which was not any of the things people said it was. Simply being different was suspect; it made you at best an oddity, at worst a pariah.

Years later, at college in Hertfordshire, halfway through my first term, a teacher told me that they had awaited my arrival in trepidation. 'We had never had someone from Dartington before.' She sounded almost disappointed that I had turned out to be a normal human being. What on earth had they expected?

And so I adapted, as people do. I learned to see the 'Where-do-you-go-to-school?' question coming from far away, and to field it before it got to me; fending it off by changing the subject or making a counter question, I got quite good at it, but there were always the persistent types who wouldn't give up, like a dog with a bone. The danger was always there, looming over me, my sword of Damocles.

And as I write this now, in the year 2008, I can still observe disapproval on the faces of people if I tell them how at my school the boys and girls swam without clothes.

'I'm sorry, but I'm afraid I don't think that is all right,' they will say.

Clearly there is something wrong with young bodies, dipping unself-consciously into a pool, or into the river which ran through the Dartington farmlands, although nothing is wrong with the fact that nowadays children in their own homes almost daily watch DVDs or TV programmes of pop singers, surrounded by young women pretending to dance, while they cavort and flaunt their sexual parts (barely concealed by black leather thongs and miniscule bras) in the most gross and lascivious manner.

When I express my distaste, I am told, 'Oh, it's the norm these days you know – everybody watches this sort of thing, even young children. It's simply the way life is now.'

So that's OK, is it? If everybody watches? So long as it is the norm, no one being different, out of the ordinary.

However, all that said, I can't say these occasional rather embarrassing reactions of strangers bothered me unduly. Much more interesting was the life going on around me, the people and surroundings I felt comfortable with, the passing years that would never again be repeated. Years when there was time and space to grow and emerge as myself, like a butterfly from a chrysalis case, among the green hills and valleys; among the fields of white morning mists, the small churches, farmyards, barns, quarries, woods and copses; the swathes of ripe cornfields in late summer. In such a setting, why care about silly opinions that weren't even true?

I was fifteen when my father decided to teach me to drive the car. He had been waiting impatiently for my sister to turn eighteen, the legal age for driving, so that he could teach her. But when that time came, to his amazement, she hadn't wanted to. He found it hard to understand how this was possible, his passion being cars – more specifically Rolls Royces. And our car, circa 1927, he cared for and cleaned and polished (the engine most particularly) with almost the same love and care that I lavished on the ponies. But I have to say that I, too, had a great affection for this roomy old car; from the time during the war when it had been laid up on bricks in the garage and had been my favourite 'toy' to play in. Now he was offering to teach me to drive it – I couldn't believe my luck.

Unable to go on public roads because of my age, we discovered an old disused race-course on the outskirts of Totnes. It hadn't seen a horse since before the war, and was unlikely to ever again. But the town council hadn't decided what use to put it to and meanwhile the whole area had been forgotten, left to run wild, weeds and grasses growing high. The track itself, washed by years of rainfall, had become hard and stony – for us it was perfect, and there it was that I grappled with starting up this huge old car, stopping, reversing and the essential art of double de-clutching.

In time, when my father considered me reasonably proficient, he would drive us to Dartmoor and once there, in places where you could see the road clear for ten miles or so, both ahead and behind, he would let me drive if there was no traffic in sight. For me, those days were glorious – driving along the narrow roads, heather, gorse and wild ponies on either side. Sometimes we would stop and go for walks and pick flowers. Other times I would invite school friends to come too, and we would visit little country tearooms for strawberry-and-cream teas. A new era of independence loomed – still far ahead but the possibilities were infinite.

At school, changes were also taking place in me, another kind of aspiration for new horizons. From being the 'terror of the hockey field' (as I alone saw myself) I was becoming dreamy and far away. Sitting out in the courtyard one afternoon – with warm summer smells of cut grass and chamomile drifting around – our English teacher, Raymond O'Malley, or Malley as we called him, read and discussed with us Matthew Arnold's *The Scholar-Gypsy*, and another time Gerard Manley Hopkins' *Pied Beauty* – and altered my life. He, Malley, would never have known it, as indeed neither did I, but a random seed was sown. I can date my gradually acquired but lifelong love of literature from then.

Summer nights, open windows, my wisteria-scented room. Late, very late, I would hear trains down below in the valley, roaring through the station and then out into the country and far beyond. Long drawn-out whistles fading slowly into the night air. Silence again. Trains to and trains from the great world outside. In my bed – it was still my cocoon – I would feel little tremors, but of what? Fear? Anticipation of adventure? Excitement? Reluctance even? For I didn't want to leave my home.

But still trains came and went, steaming between the trees along by the river, leaving white clouds suspended in branches, slowly disintegrating. And when I heard the shrill whistles in the night I invariably felt that life was beckoning me, expecting me, waiting for me – if not now, then later. There was something inevitable, even relentless in that piercing sound and I seemed to know that sooner or later the outside call would prove too strong. And I would wonder sometimes if there was perhaps an inner knowledge in everyone of what was to come. Did a pre-ordained life await me? Or would I just find my way a step at a time?

And I would think about how there were people somewhere 'out there' – already born and living their lives, as I was living mine – whom one day I would meet and get to know. And that people were not always as straight forward as they seemed, you had to learn about them. People could be puzzling.

I had begun to discover this some years back when we had briefly employed a housekeeper, a woman called Florence (the same name as my ballet teacher, but different in every way). This Florence was my friend; she liked listening to my talk about horses and cowboys and Red Indians. She liked my cat, Cassa, too, and was amused when I told her that Cassa sometimes slept on Russet's back; how I would find her in the mornings with her eyes still shut tight and her paws tucked in under her – and Russet taking care not to make sudden movements.

It was through Florence that I learned you could not expect from one person what you would expect from another, and at the time it had been confusing. She was continually promising things and not doing them. Like saying she would make me a Red Indian tunic and trousers on her sewing machine, from some old sacks I had found. She probably didn't realise how much I wanted them, how I felt my life would be somehow complete if I could ride around like an Indian with a few feathers in my hair. And although she reminded me of her kind intentions from time to time – and I would thank her gratefully and hopefully – she never actually got around to carrying them out. I had waited patiently, rather surprised, for this was a new sort of behaviour. Up until then I had only been used to the ways of my father – for whom yes meant yes, no meant no, and if he said he would do something, you knew that he would do it. As simple as that, and a sort of security, for you felt sure about things.

Florence had decamped suddenly, precipitously, leaving us with a large phone bill for calls to America. Apparently she had an American GI man friend, and had gone to be with him.

My father had laughed and said, 'She certainly was a character.' I was shocked. 'But the phone bill, it's the same as stealing, isn't it?'

'Yes, it is. But she wouldn't have thought so. She never took anything from the house, although she could have done, she had the opportunity.' My father was struggling now. He could see the question marks on my face. 'But, well look, when people fall in love, they become irrational.'

'What's irrational?'

'A little mad.'

'Oh.' I tried to look as if I understood.

'Florence wasn't a bad person,' he said, seeing my uncertain expression. 'She just wanted to be with this man. I hope he's worth it.'

Clearly there was a lot for me to learn about the adult world, but just now I was in no hurry. I preferred to let things filter through slowly, and then spend my time digesting them. I didn't want lots of facts, shocks, disillusionments coming at me bim, bam, boom – because I felt instinctively that they could undermine, even negate, what was basically essential to me, all that I held inside me; timeless, delicate and my own. I didn't want ugliness or uncertainties to intrude.

As for my social life, it was good enough. I had uncomplicated friendships with girls I had grown up with, I felt as comfortable with the boys at school as I would a pair of old boots, and now and then as I met new people, a vague kind of mutual interest might arise. Anything more than that I was prepared to shelve for the time being.

And now, looking back, what do I remember most clearly about that time? Well, I can recall as if it were yesterday, walking through the beech woods near my home, bluebells and pink campions underfoot, the smell of wild garlic all around. Or riding by the river on warm summer evenings, the occasional, unexpected moments of a kind of sublimity – a sudden glimpse of silver as a salmon leapt and twisted in the air; the brilliance of a kingfisher's blue wing; a heron standing in the shallows, silent and immobile. Sometimes I would dismount and sit on a fallen tree or a grass bank where kingcups grew half-submerged in the water - and watch dragonflies hovering and skimming over the surface of the river. On an extra good day, one of the local young farmers might ride by, greet me by name and stop for a few words. Mostly they would be on plain, strong hunters, but one of them had an eye for a horse and he always rode a bay thoroughbred. I liked them, they were different from other young men around the neighbourhood. I liked their manner; their slow smiles and quiet dignity. They had an air of assurance that came, I believe, from generations of working with the soil, the land; being at one with their work and their surroundings.

Afterwards I would ride home with a lift in my spirits, affirmed as a young woman, perhaps a little proud that they seemed to like me too.

As I have mentioned, the world around us was changing fast, and at first we were unaware of it. We were too young to see that as the exigencies of wartime receded and became a memory, fading with each year that passed, the desire to get on and do well was dividing people. At first it was just comfort and security that everyone craved, a natural reaction from the dark years of uncertainty and fear. But then, with the ambition to acquire more possessions, achieve higher social standing, ideas about success and the future were taking precedence in people's minds. And in communities all over Britain, something was becoming lost – a kindness and solidarity perhaps? For to go up, others had to go down: class consciousness was reasserting itself, coming out from the closet where it had lain, irrelevant, at least cut down to size, by rationing and the shared tragedies of bombing, or the sudden dreaded arrival of telegrams from the war office – which had affected rich and poor alike.

Dartington school too was changing beyond anything one could have imagined possible. The catalyst for this seems to have been a brief period of fame; serious articles appearing in such newspapers as *The Observer* and *The Manchester Guardian*, hailing the school as way ahead of its time, and praising it for an ethos that other schools would do well to emulate.

Shortly after I had left school, abroad at the time, I read these articles. I also heard of the death of our loved and respected headmaster. Later I was to learn how these two events transformed what had been an almost timeless way of life. Now, thanks to the extravagant media praise and sudden attention the school was getting, and the loss of Curry (who would certainly not have altered the school in any way to accommodate its new status) it gradually acquired a reputation for being trendy. Film stars, celebrities and the super-rich were sending their children to the senior school – and because they had not had the benefit of coming through the junior and middle schools, they brought with them all their entrenched attitudes and opinions from the outside world, as well as unlimited ready cash, expensive possessions and gear, and of course the latest drug culture that was pervading Britain.

The new heads of the school, a series of them one after the other, being keen to live up to expectation in the outside world, introduced programmes such as 'personality development courses' and other such outlandish concepts probably from the USA, as would have appalled Curry, being against all he believed in. Fees per child rocketed beyond the resources of any ordinary family; even the teachers in the school could no longer afford to have their own children attend. Obviously the old system of workers' children being welcomed free was long gone.

All in all the world of Dartington as we knew it, and the spirit of the school which had been created under the stewardship of Bill Curry, had been totally dismantled and replaced with a phony counterfeit, grotesque to those who knew the old ways. Now only the name and the buildings and ancient lands remained the same.

It was inevitable of course that the school (as it had become, with its vanity, self-consciousness and 'anything-goes' modern trendy-ness) should self-destruct. One scandal after another – mainly of the drug/alcohol related variety – brought it so low, time and again, repeatedly, that it was finally closed down.

And now, when people ask me where I went to school and I reply, '*Dartington*,' – it's the same old story. They stare and say, 'Not Dartington: Isn't that the school that got closed down?'

And I haven't the appetite to explain – I merely reply, 'Yes, that's the one.

For how could I make them understand; convey in a few words how it was all the years when I was there? Their minds are made up, and I am obliged to listen while they say, almost triumphantly (for there is something threatening about freedom), 'Oh well, it was an experiment that didn't work.'

The fact that it did work, quite exceptionally well (for which I am immeasurably grateful) until the outside world moved in and violated all it stood for, is only known by a few. A knowledge that in time will be gone forever. Gone silently, disintegrating like the morning mists rising up from the river at the start of a new day.

As for Totnes, my home town, a way of life there too was passing away, as all things do and must. Post war changes brought tourism, first in a trickle and then big time. As visitors to the south started to arrive in droves – mostly northerners touring Devon and Cornwall for holidays – our once quiet, agricultural market town became particularly favoured, singled out for its picturesque beauty; its steep narrow Fore Street, the Guildhall, Butterwalk and Castle. In no time small slate-roofed town houses and nearby thatched farm cottages were being bought up by outsiders for prices unaffordable by local young couples.

On the other hand, boutiques and souvenir shops opened, small businesses and local craft centres were set up and although the essential nature of the area changed, new life was injected into the community which has continued to flourish, even to lead the way in methods of self-reliant living – as a transition town, facing modern challenges. And it is comforting to know that the River Dart still flows through the town, under the stone bridge and on down to Dartmouth.

For myself, I too got swept this way and that by the winds of change. On my last day at school, our headmaster, Curry, came and put his arm around me and said, 'Well, Janet, you've been with us since you were three years old – we're going to miss you!'

Only then did the enormity of the fracture become reality, and I couldn't contain my tears.

After that it was college in Hertfordshire, travel and then work in refugee camps, under the UNICEF Aid to Refugees Programme. This was 1956, the year of the unsuccessful Hungarian revolt against the occupying Russian communist forces. Like most unarmed uprisings it started small, but the soviet reaction of sending tanks into Budapest unleashed a long-suppressed fury – followed by bloody confrontation and the subsequent headlong flight of thousands of refugees.

I remained committed to this work – duly acquiring a newborn Hungarian godson – until unwisely, unwittingly and far too young, I married someone I believed to be a naval officer in the British Royal Navy, but who instead turned out to be a KGB spy – but that's another story.

In this memoir I have tried to build up, through a series of perhaps insignificant incidents, as if painted with small brush strokes, a picture of a time now passed away. And from what I have recalled and written about, I can see clearly that the most valuable thing I gained from my early life was not academic, not qualifications that would ensure a high salary, but the knowledge that if anything can get us through this hard life, it is having had a decent childhood.

After leaving Dartington, Janet attended Ashridge House of Citizenship for one year and then led an interesting and well travelled life. After the Hungarian revolution she volunteered with Hungarian refugees near Marlborough in Wiltshire. At the age of twenty she married a South African naval officer and moved to South Africa with him. The marriage broke down after some years and she returned to the UK. Her husband was eventually exposed as a Soviet spy. She later wrote a book about the experience, called The Spy's Wife. While living in Ireland she wrote three novels set in Dublin. She also lived in Greece for a while, where she taught English and collaborated with a leading Greek poet Zissimos Lorenzatos on a translation into English of a classic Greek novel. She later married, a Greek academic, Costas Balis, and went to live in Tasmania for two years. Back in Ireland, single again, she taught pottery in Dunshane, a Camphill community thirty miles outside Dublin. In later years she moved to be near her daughter Ingrid and her son Tom and their families near Edinburgh.

Janet died in 2010 in Edinburgh.